THE
FOUNDATION STONE MEDITATION

A New Commentary

Adrian Anderson   PhD

Copyright: Adrian Anderson
Threshold Publishing
Melbourne
Australia

www.rudolfsteinerstudies.com

Digital Distribution by Ebook Alchemy

ISBN 9780958134118

All rights reserved

© **2007,** revised 2023

CONTENTS

1 Introduction

2 The foundation stone ceremony and speech.   7
An esoteric address given by Rudolf Steiner at the laying of the foundation stone of the first Goetheanum in 1913.

3 Re-founding the Anthroposophical Society in 1923.   16

4 The Foundation Stone verse: 20
  a: introductory remarks
  b: a new translation of the complete text

5 The Placing of the Foundation Stone: lecture   40
of 25th Dec. 1923: a new, annotated translation, designed to make this difficult, inspired text more understandable.

6 Commentary on the Verse   55

7 The German text of the verse   94

Illustrations
1 The copper double dodecahedron
2 A geometric sketch of his copper form
3 The foundation parchment and its inscription
4 A diagram of the seven 'members' of the nine Hierarchies and of the human being

Other books by the Author

Introduction

The Anthroposophical Society was founded on February 3rd in 1913, in a conference held in Berlin on the 3rd to 7th February of that year. Its executive consisted of Rudolf Steiner (as honorary president), Marie von Sivers, Michael Bauer and Carl Unger. Some 2,557 people, previously Theosophists, joined the newly founded Anthroposophical Society. Plans to erect a building to serve as the centre for this new Society, which could also host international conferences, had already been discussed, and explored for the town of Munich. This proved not possible under the building requirements of the city's council. The present site in Dornach, near Basel, was donated, and architectural plans drawn up.

The new society, the Anthroposophical Society, that was formed in response to the impulse of spiritual renewal that Rudolf Steiner inaugurated, began the task of building a centre for anthroposophical work. Some form of foundation stone ceremony was expected, as this was part of the cultural tradition of central Europe.

However Rudolf Steiner deepened the meaning of this traditional ceremony by imbuing it with profoundly esoteric qualities. When the first such ceremony took place, in 1913, a physical foundation stone was placed in the ground, and the building was then constructed over that site. In 1923, when Rudolf Steiner deemed it necessary to re-found the Anthroposophical Society, a spiritual 'foundation stone' was laid in the hearts of the members.

The first foundation stone of the building that was about to be erected for the Anthroposophical Society was not a polished stone slab, placed very visibly in the wall, it was a symbolic object made of copper, and placed out of sight under the ground. Work on this building commenced in September 1913. The photograph shown here of this copper dodecahedron form was published by the craftsman who constructed it following Rudolf Steiner's specifications.[1]

Illustration One

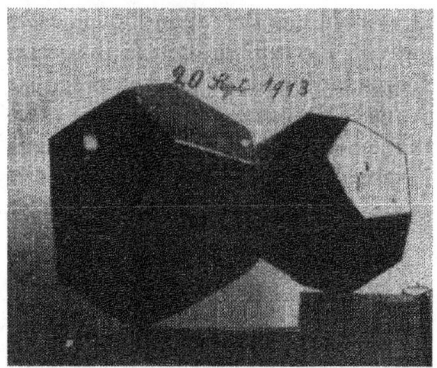

The specially constructed foundation stone, inside a protective receptacle, was to be put in a hollow concrete block (1.2m x 1m x 70cm), and ceremoniously placed in the ground. It was to be lowered into a small excavation on a hill in Dornach. Work would then start on the building which was to become the international centre for anthroposophy. The site of the foundation stone would be underneath the small cupola.

It was intended to call this building The Johannes Building (more idiomatically in English, the St. John's

---

[1] The copper form was made by Max Benzinger, who included this photo in his article, "Ein Augenzeuge der Grundsteinlegung berichtet." published in Mitteilungen aus der anthroposophischen Arbeit in Deutschland, Stuttgart; 1963, Michaelmas.

Building), but following the suggestion of an English member of the Society, Rudolf Steiner changed this to *The Goetheanum*, in honour of Johann Wolfgang von Goethe. The Foundation Stone is a double twelve-sided form (dodecahedron) made from copper, one form is smaller (54cm) than the other (63cm). It is still there today, underneath the new Goetheanum.

This form was intended to symbolize the human soul as a microcosm emerging from the spiritual world, the macrocosm. Rudolf Steiner's explanation of this form, delivered in a ceremonial speech, is given later (p.13). The above photograph shows it resting on a wooden support, on the day it was to be placed in the soil. This double-form is similar to the basic design of the Goetheanum with its two cupolas, the smaller one emerging from the larger. It is interesting to note that inside the copper foundation stone, two iron pyrites crystals were suspended.

The larger crystal (30 mm x 20 mm) is inside the smaller copper dodecahedron, the smaller crystal (25mm x 15mm) inside the larger dodecahedron. The requirement that two iron pyrites crystals be placed inside the double dodecahedron copper form was never directly explained, nor indeed, even mentioned formally by Rudolf Steiner. However, in an article about this foundation stone, Ernst Bindel reports that in a private conversation Rudolf Steiner indicated that suspending these rocks inside a copper form in the shape of a dodecahedron had an supportive influence on the capacity of both the cupolas to resist the force of gravity.[2] The shape of the pyrites crystal is a pentagonal dodecahedron.

---

[2] Ernst Bindel, "Die sinnbildiche Bedeutung des Pentagon-Dodekaeders als Grundstein geistig bedeutsamer Bauten" in

The work on these various items, and the concreting of the small excavation which was to receive the wooden casing in which the foundation stone was to be placed, was completed on September 20th 1913. However the exact day and time of the ceremony in which the foundation stone which would be sealed inside the casing, and then lowered into soil, had been kept secret. At 7pm on September 20th, Rudolf Steiner let it be known that the event was to commence immediately, and a group of excited members gathered at the site as word spread.

The text of his words, accompanied by a simple ritual, was kept confidential for decades. But in 1976 this text was made public by Rudolf Grosse, a member of the Dornach 'Vorstand', in his book, "Die Weihnachtstagung als Zeitenwende".[3] I am including this text here, in the understanding that these words provide an immensely valuable context for understanding and thus meditating with the Foundation Stone verse.

Rudolf Steiner spoke in the dark night, against the wind and rain, under a make-shift tent, on the muddy site of the future Goetheanum. It was nearly the autumn equinox, that season when the Archangel Michael becomes the predominant guiding force spirtiually for the hemisphere's elemental forces. The site was illumined by a wood fire and by some pitch torches held aloft by a few people. Nearby was the copper foundation stone, and the

---

Mitteilungen aus der anthroposophischen Arbeit in Deutschland, Stuttgart; Christmas 1956, no. 38.
[3] "The Christmas Foundation Conference as a turning-point of time." Published by Philosophisch-Anthroposophischer Verlag, Dornach, 1976.

casing block, and the excavation in which a concrete plinth had been placed.

In giving this address to the assembled group, Rudolf Steiner referred to the esoteric meaning of this copper dodecahedron, which provides invaluable help in understanding many of the allusions in the 1923 Foundation Stone verse. In addition to this copper "stone" a white calf-skin parchment on which a graphic design and a brief esoteric text was written was placed inside the block.

In the ceremony, Rudolf Steiner also described in a general way what was written on the parchment, however he did not state exactly the text as written. In the next section, this document is reproduced, and its exact text is translated in full.

Illustration Two

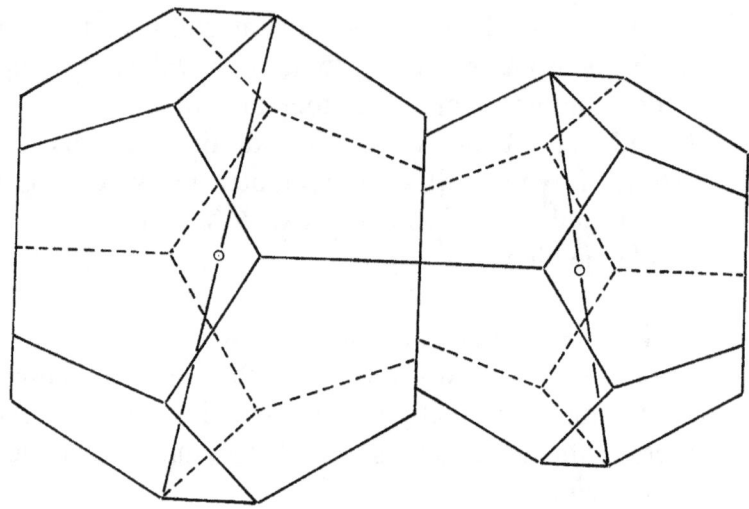

A geometrical drawing of the double dodecahedral copper, showing the two pyrites crystals suspended inside each dodecahedron and the pentagonal shape of each facet. Published in "Die Weihnachtstagung als Zeitenwende" by Rudolf Grosse, p.44. This 12-fold structure is to be thought of as underlying the two form of the cupolas of the first Goetheanum.

2 The Foundation Stone ceremony and speech:
an esoteric address spoken at 7pm at the laying of the foundation stone for the Goetheanum in Dornach, on September 20th, 1913.

" We begin our work !"
((*Turning to the east, south, west and north, at each of these points he named one of the ranks of hierarchical beings.*[4]))
You *Cherubim*, you *Seraphim* – you guiders of worlds, and you *Thrones* who, like lightning throughout the streams of spiritual forces, absorb the sheaths of the Cherubim, uniting them to the creative existence of the cosmos —
we invoke you as guardians of our ritual deed.

And you *Wisdoms*, who have created in humanity all that which is so particularly its inner being;
and you, *Preservers* of the eternal cosmic forces,
and you, who *form* our existence, who place the form of all being within the streams of existence – we invoke you as protectors of our actions.

And you *Personalities* of the spiritual streams, and you Helpers, the Archangels and the Angels, who are the messengers of the spiritual life of humanity for the Earth – all you we invoke as those who are protecting and guiding this, our deed.
We invoke you upon the human soul, whom we wish to consecrate, in so far as that lies within our ability. We now approach this human soul, whom we wish to consecrate to the work which is intended

---

[4] In German the following invocation used the very evocative 2nd person plural, which in English is "ye".

to serve you spirits, to the best of our understanding of the times.

We have dedicated this stone, as a symbol of the human soul, who is undertaking our Great Work.[5] To us, in its double twelve-fold shape, it is a symbol of the human soul, which is striving as a microcosm immersed in the macrocosm: Anthropos, the human soul – in its origin from the beings of the divine-spiritual hierarchies. Thus, this our corner stone is the symbol of our own soul, which we wish to place within that which we recognize as the right spiritual striving for the present times.

So, we shall lower this stone, which has been formed according to the cosmic images of the human soul, into the realm of the elements. Within this stone there are two rocks, taken from the densified[6] realm of the elements, which best bring to expression how macrocosmic forces work together in their efficacy within the densified realm of the elements.[7]

This twelve-foldness – we shall lower into the soil this evening, as the actual symbol of the human soul; at that location above which shall be erected what will become a symbol to us of our efficacy, once we have rightly understood this, my dear theosophical friends.[8]

---

[5] The expression, "Great Work" has a specific context; it was used in esoteric circles of medieval Europe, such as alchemical and Rosicrucian. It refers in general to the initiatory process of building a 'house' for deity; thus a temple like that of Solomon, or one's soul as vessel for the spirit; and these two meanings are also interconnected.
[6] I have coined the word "densified" here, to express the subtle meaning of the German word, 'verdichtet'.
[7] That is, these crystals are dodecahedral in shape.
[8] The term, 'anthroposophists' or 'anthroposophers' was not yet in use, the new Society had only been founded six months earlier.

And with this stone, we are also placing a document in the ground, through which we have pledged ourselves to what we have recognized as the truly right stream in the spiritual life of our times.

This document – it will be placed inside our stone. It bears the inscription:

> **In the name of the Seraphim, the Cherubim, the Thrones, the {spirits of} Wisdom, the {spirits of} Movement, the {spirits of} Form, the Archai, the Archangels, the Angels:**
> **The human being lives as a microcosm in the macrocosm – anthropos,** [9]

who is also portrayed here {on the parchment} as a twice twelve-fold image, symbol of the spiritual world.[10]

And within this symbol there is portrayed, my dear theosophical friends, the well-known saying of the Rosicrucians which expresses the purpose of our striving:

Ex Deo Nascimur   In Christo Morimur
Per Spiritum Sanctum Reviviscimus [11]

---

[9] The text has the odd expressions, "the Wisdoms, the Movers, the Formers", I am assuming here that the full, correct designations, coined by Rudolf Steiner himself, were spoken, but this is not certain. The text was written down by light of a pitch torch, on a piece of paper which was supported, against the wind, on the moist jacket of a friend standing in front of the writer.

[10] The reason for the human soul being regarded as 5-fold and as 12-fold shall be examined later.

[11] The text here has the abbreviations of these three phrases, but I am assuming the these phrases were spoken. The phrases mean "From God we are born", "Into Christ we die" and, "By the Holy Spirit we are resurrected".

Let us rightly understand what we are doing – on this stone, as our corner-stone, there is also stated as the wording of our vow –

**the human being who wills to –
seek itself in Spirit
feel itself in the Soul of the Cosmos
intuit itself in the I of the Cosmos.**

**This stone we now place down in the densified realm of the elements
as a symbol of the Power towards which we are seeking to strive, through
...three, five, seven, twelve** [12]

Placed by the St. John's Building[13] **Association, Dornach on the 20**[th] **day of September 1880, after the Mystery of Golgotha; i.e., 1913 AD, as Mercury stood in Libra as the evening star.**

**As builder: Carl Schmidt-Curtius
As board of the St. John's Building Association:
Stinde, Linde, Kalkreuth, Gumppenberg, Schieb, Großheintz,**

Peipers, Bürgi, Hirter-Weber.

As central executive of Anthroposophical Society: von Sivers, Unger

---

[12] Rudolf Steiner spoke these numbers, and later struck the copper dodecahedron that number of times.

[13] Literally, the Johannes Building Association, but St. John is perhaps the more correct English rendering.

As spiritual director of the deed: Rudolf Steiner

This document will be incorporated into the symbol of the human soul, and then into the densified realm of the elements.

((*The document was rolled up and placed inside the receptacle in which the copper foundation stone was lying. Then M. Benzinger soldered the lid onto the receptacle.*))

The stone, the symbol of our soul, will be placed down into the densified realm of the elements.

((*Then the receptacle, with the foundation stone and parchment inside, was carried by Dr. Felix Peipers, from behind, at the larger part. He was assisted by two other men at each side (Linde and Bürgi, Großheintz and Schmidt) using long belts, crossed over each other. It was lowered in the hole, and placed on the plinth, so that the larger dodecahedron lies to the east, the smaller towards the west. That is, the opposite configuration of the two cupolas of the building itself.*))

The stone, the symbol of our soul has been placed into the earth. May it be an emblem of the striving for knowledge, for Love, for strong action – the symbol of humanity. For our souls it should become an emblem of that which always resounds from the deepest meaning of the cosmic word:
Ex Deo nascimur. In Christo morimur. Per Spiritum Sanctum reviviscimus.

From this *symbol* of the human soul there should arise a *sign* of the human soul. I consecrate you as a *sign* of the human soul with the first blows which are to be made in this, our real building:

(*three, five and seven blows are made on the smaller, and twelve blows on the larger part*)

From being previously a symbol, the stone has herewith become a *sign*. And now we want to entrust it to the realm of the densified elements, the Earth, into which our soul has been immersed, in order to develop in humanity's evolution that which is the mission of the Earth to develop. In that we are entrusting the stone to the Earth, this stone which has become a sign, now becomes something *enveloped, veiled*.

Human souls arise in three stages to the secrets of existence. Firstly these (spiritual truths) are symbols, and then they are signs, in which the soul reads the eternal Cosmic-Word. Then the deepest depths of the cosmic secrets become united livingly with the soul – when the soul is able to give to itself an integument {a veil} from the realm of the hierarchies.[14]

So become enveloped !

Something veiled will develop from the sign and the symbol, which then becomes a 'veiler' itself; in order that you, O stone, may become a solid corner-stone of our striving, our seeking.[15]

---

[14] These three brief descriptions equate with the three stages are higher consciousness. The spiritual worlds appear firstly as symbols (Imagination) to the meditant, then one reads the Cosmic Script (Inspiration), finally one attains to a union with the Spiritual.

[15] It is to be regretted that the English language has lost the use of its more intimate address forms, i.e. thou and ye. For these are essential to express certain matters. The 2nd person singular was used here

So, we want to bring a veiled condition over our stone, which is a sign of our soul.

((Fraulein von Sivers places a bouquet of roses, consisting of 12 red and one white rose, on the copper foundation stone. Architect Schmidt and engineer Engler cover it with soil. Thereupon Dr. Steiner shakes the hands, cross-wise, of those present at the site of the foundation stone: Dr. F. Peipers, Dr. Großheintz, architect Schmidt and engineer Engler. Then everyone leaves the excavated hole, a wooden board is then placed over the hole and it is covered entirely with soil.))

Rudolf Steiner then addressed the gathering briefly, speaking about the mission of anthroposophy to express the will of the cosmic Christ, who is now united to the soul of the Earth. No further specific references to the symbolism or nature of the foundation stone were made in that speech.

(i.e., 'thou stone') because remarkably, Rudolf Steiner now addresses the stone directly as if it were a living being, and also as if this person or being was also an important intimate known friend.

Illustration Three

The white parchment which was placed with the copper dodecahedron

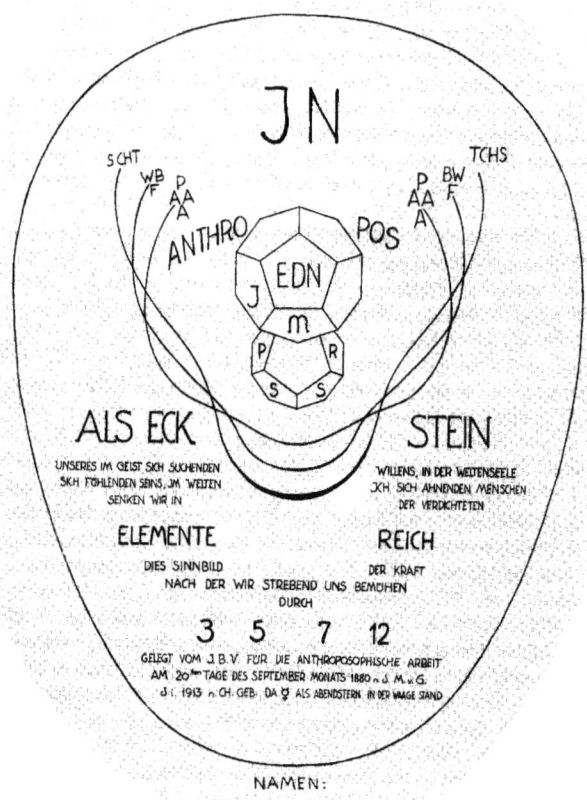

On the page opposite is a translation of the inscription on this document. This illustration was published in Rudolf Grosse, "Die Weihnachtstagung als Zeitenwende".

J N   (ie Jesus of Nazareth)

(The initials of the nine ranks of hierarchical beings are given twice, left and right of the 'face':

S(eraphim) Ch(erubim) T(hrones)
W(isdom) B(Movement) F(orm)
P(rincipalities) AA(rchangel) A (ngel).

(In the centre of the image are the Rosicrucian initials, although the letter 'c' for Christ is omitted. Above these letters is the word)   'anthropos'.

As Corner Stone

of our will (which is) seeking itself in the Spirit, our being (which is) feeling-sensing itself in the soul of the cosmos, our human self (which is) intuiting itself in the I of the cosmos -- we place into the

densified realm of the elements

this symbol of the power through which we towards which we are seeking to strive, through,

$$3 \quad 5 \quad 7 \quad 12$$

Placed by the St. John's Building Association, for the anthroposophical work, on the 20th day of September 1880, after the Mystery of Golgotha; i.e., 1913 AD, as Mercury stood in Libra as the evening star.

Names:

3. The Re-founding of the Anthroposophical Society in Christmas 1923

During the following decade anthroposophy became increasingly tangible as a welcome force towards social and personal renewal, but hostility to it also grew, and in January 1921, a religious organization, infamous for its aggression and political machinations, threatened to burn down the Goetheanum. Following Rudolf Steiner's urgent request that the building be protected, efforts were made to put in place defensive measures, although lack of services and general infrastructure in the area made this a difficult task.

In fact, tragically, one year later, on the night of the 31st Dec 1921 to 1st Jan 1922, the Goetheanum was indeed burnt down. One of the greatest architectural achievements of all civilisations, a priceless gift of European esoteric-spiritual life, the centre for a renewal of the cultural-artistic life, and the visible sign of the re-establishing the Mysteries for modern humanity, was gone. Plans for a second building made of concrete were drawn up, and after Rudolf Steiner's death this building was constructed.

During 1923 Rudolf Steiner focussed in his lectures on the need to address the imperfections in the Anthroposophical Society that had weakened its social and spiritual functioning. The lack of the physical building, and the need to replace it was a primary focus of attention. As became obvious later in the Christmas Re-Founding Conference, Rudolf Steiner was contemplating carrying out a new form of the process of laying the foundation-stone, quite different to the ritualistic placing in the soil of a physical object. The

Anthroposophical Society was to be re-founded in the initial days of a nine-day conference in the Christmas-Yuletide time. The invitation specifically stated that the first two days, Dec 24th and 25th, would be especially important, as Rudolf Steiner would be giving the guidelines for the Christmas Conference and the future work; and also in these days, the new 'international' Anthroposophical Society would receive its consecration.

The intention was to place the foundation stone of the future anthroposophical work in the hearts of the members. Additionally, the executive would be extended to include six people, each to be responsible for an area of human endeavour to which the anthroposophical movement could offer a renewal. The fields mentioned during the conference were, education, literary pursuits, science, the arts and general anthroposophy. Later, others were added to this list.

When the Foundation Stone meditation was given there were about 700 people present, members of the Society from around the world. They were there as part of the Christmas Re-founding of the Anthroposophical Society. This conference took place in the northern hemisphere's Yuletide or Holy Nights period of 1923/24. The winter-solstice Yuletide period of either hemisphere, is a time when sacred spiritual forces are present in the hemisphere's aura.

Members of the Esoteric School – an institution within the Society through which Rudolf Steiner offered guidance in meditation and higher development – were informed that the Yuletide or Holy Nights period (of either hemisphere) is a time of special importance. It had been revealed in the School that at this time of the year, the high initiates or "Masters" as they are called in Theosophy, are active with exceptionally sacred forces that arise through the hemisphere's winter in-breath. These forces are connected closely with the cosmic Christ.

Rudolf Steiner spoke the verse on Christmas day 1923 for the first time, and then gave some indications as to its meaning. The text of this address is a remarkable document; it shows clearly the degree of inspiration under which he was speaking. Apart from this address, only a few brief passages about the verse were spoken during the nine-day conference.

Furthermore, on the nine occasions when he spoke the verse, it was often in an incomplete form. This lecture is the one place where Rudolf Steiner speaks the verse in its entirety and also provides a commentary. By meditating on the very condensed statements in the Foundation Stone meditation, one forms a deep link to the threefold divine reality that it proclaims: the Trinity without, and its reflection within the human being.

Through the meditative process these truths also become indissolubly linked to one's own being. They become one's own wisdom, and begin to transform the soul spiritually, by uniting it to the sacred source of spirituality, which flows through the anthroposophical movement, access to which was inaugurated by Rudolf Steiner. Rudolf Steiner later revealed that during the conference, he became aware of the spiritual presence of the sublime high initiate Christian Rosenkreutz, who by his presence was affirming the decision to re-found the Anthroposophical Society.

The First Goetheanum was a building so remarkable and architecturally so great that it – and its designer and the artisans who worked to build it – cannot be adequately honoured here. However, being constructed of wood, it was vulnerable to the work of arsonists. Its interior form was intended to speak to humanity of the spiritual origins of the human being, and of the living interconnection of the human being, as a microcosm, with the macrocosmic spiritual nexus. The Goetheanum was also designed to communicate these truths through the resonance it had with speech and artistic creativity.

The form of the first Goetheanum with its double cupolas was embodied in the shape of its remarkable foundation stone. Much effort was made to embody the qualities of the first building in the second Goetheanum, which is constructed of concrete. But in the context of a differently shaped building, the unique virtue of the first building could not be fully realized. However the present Goetheanum has recently been beautifully renovated, with the focus on completing the artistic element, making it also a wonderful architectural experience.

4 : The Foundation Stone Verse
Some preliminary remarks are necessary concerning my the choice of English terms. The following translation is accurate and literary, however I have not always found it possible to retain the structural form of the original. This is the most comprehensive meditative text given by Rudolf Steiner, and therefore some commentary on the use of English terms for German expressions is necessary.

A major reason for the Foundation Stone meditation not being extensively used, is the difficulty of understanding the meaning of various phrases in it. Since the implications of these phrases are at times obscure in the German original, the ambiguity can intensify when it is translated. In the translation given here, all phrases have a clear meaning, and are accurate to the original text. I have been helped by my work with the Esoteric School material, and the First Class material over the past quarter century.

The most noticeable example of the confusion with regard to words, is perhaps a phrase at the beginning of section D. In most translations, we find the sentence in English, "At the turning-point of time, *the Spirit-light of the World* entered the stream of earthly being". This is incorrect, as the event referred to here concerns an entering into the Earth of a specific divine Being, designated by Rudolf Steiner as from 1904, as the "Welten-Geist".

This German phrase is grammatically ambiguous, but from the context of its usage in esoteric material, it is correct translation is confirmed as, *the Spirit of the Cosmos*. Hence the correct translation is, "At the

20

turning-point of time, the light of the Cosmos-Spirit entered the stream of earthly being." The *Spirit of the Cosmos* is a name given by Rudolf Steiner to an extremely important spiritual Being; whereas the translation, "The spirit-light of the world" has virtually no meaning. However, a definition of the being designated by this phrase, the "Welten-Geist" is apparently only to be found in material associated with esoteric lessons of 1904, and hence this phrase has remained enigmatic until those texts were accessed.[16] The nature of the Being referred to as the "Welten-Geist", and its association to the Christ, is explained in the commentary.

The commentary following my translation is intended to be a brief guide, giving through its contemplative, aphoristic style, a stimulus to meditative engagement with the verse. It is important to note that Rudolf Steiner recommended that specific, small sections of the long four-fold verse be especially meditated upon each day. These seven sections are clearly identified in the special version of my translation. Naturally one should contemplate the entire text at regular intervals, in order to have it livingly in one's mind. How often this is done is up to each person, because the individual is treated as an individual in this path.

---

[16] Over the past 20 years I have carefully worked with these 220 lessons (the essence of these lessons, regarding the meditative path, are in my book, *The Way to the Sacred*).

The words, "efficacy" and "efficacious" – replacing the words, "reign" or "rule" or "hold sway".

In order to enter into understanding of this profound and condensed meditative text, we have to make use of some words that are rarely used today, as no other English term conveys the meaning of the German. These words may have to be freed of nuances of meaning that they acquired from other contexts. In this great verse, a triune source of divine creativity and the reflection of this in the human being – in body and soul and spirit – is the most important underlying context. But the concept of a Trinity of divine creators has a potent ecclesiastical ambience, which has been acquired over centuries.

In an esoteric context, the attitude to "God" or to the Trinity in general is quite different to that in exoteric religious circles. Earlier translators were not sufficiently aware of their unconscious universe of discourse, and they also worked without the advantage, available to us today, of accessing the 360 volumes of Rudolf Steiner's complete works. It appears that some phrases have been translated with an incorrect nuance, despite great care being taken.

The Foundation Stone meditation is an important part of the inner life of those seeking to tread the path to self-initiation within the anthroposophical stream. To meditate with this verse, it is essential to have an understanding of Rudolf Steiner's perspective regarding the primal divine creator Beings. The following comments are entirely intended to assist the reader, they are not in anyway intended to enter into dialogue with ecclesiastical pronouncements.

The nature of God, indeed of the three beings of the Trinity, as experienced, and consequently taught, by the high initiate Rudolf Steiner, is very definitely not an all-powerful, 'monarchical' authority against whose intentions no other being can prevail. That is, in anthroposophical initiation wisdom, neither God nor the Christ nor the Holy Spirit are "all-powerful", nor "almighty". The expression "Almighty God" is very clearly viewed as an error by Rudolf Steiner. He elucidated the nature of God in various lectures, and specifically rejected the concept of God as 'almighty'.

There are only a few places where he writes about Natural Theology (the philosophical contemplation of deity and Its relationship to humanity). In one of these, Rudolf Steiner teaches that God is the 'Weltengrund', meaning the substratum, basis or foundational element of the cosmos; an expression which is scarcely translatable directly into English. He states that,

> "God (Weltengrund) has fully poured out Himself into the cosmos; He has not withdrawn from it in order to guide it from outside. Rather He impels it from within, He has not withheld Himself from it. The highest mode of His manifestation within the reality of normal existence is (human) thinking and through this factor, the human personality.
>
> Thus if God has goals, then they are identical with the goals that human beings set themselves, as He lives within these. But this does not occur through the human being trying to investigate one of other command of the Regent of the cosmos, and acting according to such a goal. It occurs through the human being acting from his or her own understanding.
>
> For within these is living this Regent of the cosmos. He does not exist as Will somewhere outside of the human being; for he has forgone such a will of his own, in order to make

everything dependent upon the will of the human being.[17]

In lectures about Christmas and about the mission of the great Archangel Michael, Rudolf Steiner clarified these teachings, teaching that God does not have absolute power, does not rule supreme. He referred to three great virtues, or realities, namely Wisdom, Power and Love. He explains that God can not be all-wise as that would prevent humanity attaining to true freedom, because God can only know all things if the decisions that are as yet unborn in the human soul were also known in advance.

Further, he explains that God cannot be an all-powerful (almighty) ruler, as that would also prevent human freedom. That is, such a condition prevailing in deity, would prevent humanity from manifesting its own will. As he explained, "For Love is the creative principle in the cosmos….God has retained Love, but shared Power and Wisdom with Lucifer and Ahriman.….the 'all-might' of God would exclude human freedom !"[18]

Such formulations as "almighty God, ruler of heaven and Earth" is an expression in which the normal earthly self, with its unobserved luciferic-ahrimanic shadows, projects onto deity its own very imperfect ideals and yearnings. As Rudolf Steiner emphasized, this concept arose only after the fourth century AD, before this time, God was not considered to be almighty. Rudolf Steiner acknowledges that the use of the concept of an all-powerful God is appropriate in the exoteric ecclesiastical sphere.[19] The esoteric Christian initiate knows however that God is all-loving; God is a Being of infinite

---

[17] R. Steiner, "Outlines of a theory of epistemology of the Goethean world-view" page 125 (German edition), in *Human freedom*.

[18] Lect. 17th Dec 1912 "Love and its significance in the world".

[19] The use of this phrase in the creed of Christian churches does not contradict this; but this theme can not be discussed any further here.

compassion, of infinite love or goodness of will; God is Love.

The German term "walten" was used by Rudolf Steiner when referring to the activity of the three divine 'Persons' of the Godhead; and in earlier versions of this verse it is invariably translated to mean potent authority or exercising full power. Although this German word does have this meaning, it also has other equally valid meanings, as will be examined below. Such translations as, "Where in strength sublime of world-creative life" or "Where in the wielding World-Creator-life" [20] are out of place here.

The primal meanings of 'walten' are A: to reign or rule as a monarch, but also, B: to exist, to act, in the sense of being effective, of carrying out one's tasks. From what we have considered above, namely, that God is not an absolute authority, it is clear that this word in the Foundation Stone meditation has the latter meaning, namely to be active, to effectively carry out an action, that is, to produce an effect on something. In this verse it does not mean that God is reigning or ruling. The main English word that expresses these nuances of meaning is efficacious; from the noun 'efficacy'. This word is generally defined as meaning " a capacity (for serving) to produce effects". Operative is another word for wirken.

These words are seldom used, and may sound at first odd, but we have to become familiar with them, as they are essential to express the German concept of walten (B)

---

[20] The word, 'walten' defined in various dictionaries:
1 1901 Muret: rule, hold sway, be active, exist, to act, prevail (=vorhanden sein), **2** 1909 Koehler: govern, rule, reign, manage; **3** 1909 Cassells: rule, govern, command, **4** Langenscheidt Concise 1970: govern, rule, be at work, attend to duties, working, **5** Langenscheidt/Muret 1990: prevail preside, be, hidden but effective activity **6** Pons/Collins 1999: prevail reign, be at work, **7** Oxford Duden 2000 :prevail, reign, exercise (i.e., make effective)

(and especially, Wirkung/wirken). For these terms mean to actively exercise an effective influence. Therefore 'efficacious' or 'efficacy' are especially required where there is a *spiritual* activity having an influence, not a mundane 'work', nor an powerful autocratic action. Once these words are spoken and meditated upon for a few days, they become very acceptable, their strangeness is only a passing feeling. So in my translation, the term 'efficacious' replaces 'ruling/reigning'; for example,
"For efficacious is the Father-Spirit of the Heights engendering being in the depths of the cosmos"…

This translation tells us that in the realms far removed from divine spheres, especially in the mineral-physical plane on our planet, (the 'depths of the cosmos') the Father-God is active — but not as an unopposed monarch — for the purpose of making certain dynamics effective. The intention of these dynamics is to make possible the bringing into being of an eternal spiritual reality within the human self.

Instead of humanity retaining an illusory ego, with Lucifer-Ahrimanic influences and illusions, the loving intention of God, which is being actively expressed in our sphere of existence, is that humanity, through its actions and its inner work, shall attain to the state known as Spirit-Man (the fully conscious and divinised will forces).

That is, humanity shall be able to consolidate a spiritual core in its soul, that links it to God, to the spiritual worlds. We shall then have real being within us. However to conclude that this process proceeds without any opposition, guaranteeing the outcome beforehand, is to ignore the existence of opposing powers.

These beings are also unfolding their malignant intentions in the same sphere, aiming at the same group – humanity. In the evolutionary nexus where humanity has its existence, a triune deity and demonic beings and human will all exert their influence.

Consequently, many humans may not attain to this Spirit-Man, at least, not in the scope of those evolutionary aeons which are discussed in anthroposophy. This is clear from Rudolf Steiner lectures on the Apocalypse of St. John. The freedom of the human being to participate in, or to reject this process is part of the reality of life, and hence God does not rule or hold sway as the <u>predominating</u>, that is, the really prevailing force. Incarnate people exist in the realms where evolutionary processes are active, and subject to good and evil dynamics.

A reigning or ruling God, whose actions clear the field, being the only force, the predominating power, would be a contradiction. Initiation wisdom does not put forward the idea that God is ruling over the cosmos, but rather that He is actively in existence, producing effects within creation that humanity, if it so wills, may take up into its inner being. The same dynamic is true of the Son and the Holy Spirit.[21] That my translation is correct in this matter is confirmed by a phrase in the address given by Rudolf Steiner, "The Placing of the Foundation Stone" (see next section) wherein this same word is used specifically of the dynamics of divine love (page 50).

This process of God's subtle influences in Creation unfolding their efficacy within the realms of space, and in the cycles of time, occurs without limiting our freedom. We naturally think of the eternal Higher-self as a single, one point of spiritual reality or being-ness. However when the successful meditant is granted some experience of this Self, he or she experiences that it is actually dodecahedral. The twelve-fold cosmic word issuing from

---

[21] Regarding using the word, 'prevail' for 'walten', dictionaries record this meaning only since the 1970's; that is, to be the ruling or dominant being or factor. Prevail — if it means to be the dominant force — is just another term or rule or reign. It could be used here, in the sense of 'somewhat noticeably present', but this is an incorrect use of the word.

the zodiac, imprints its signature into the Devachanic 'substance' of our spirit, and bestows on it a twelve-fold quality.

This esoteric matter of our dodecahedral Self or "I" is indicated only briefly by Rudolf Steiner in various lectures. For example, in one lecture he speaks of the twelve cosmic points from which forces flow into the human being, "Where is the actual "I" in the human being? …the human being must feel that it belongs to the cosmos….it is embedded in these twelve points…the divine-spiritual powers exert their influence upon the human being through these twelve points."[22]

This truth of our higher self is geometrically expressed in our time-cycle as a smaller dodecahedron with pentagram-shaped facets, emerging from a larger dodecahedron. The reason that each facet of the dodecahedrons is pentagram-shaped, refers to another aspect of the human being. That is, to the four-fold human being in whom the fifth element, the Spirit-Self, is developing.

The fact that the foundation stone was made of copper, the metal of Venus, has a direct relevance here. For when the geocentric path of Venus is followed, one sees that over a period of some years it forms a spiral pattern with five petals or segments to it. Venus, the planet known in classical astrology as the planet of love, is affirmed by anthroposophy as indeed that planet from whose spiritual forces both the romantic love of youth and a higher love associated with spiritualized soul qualities have their origin. One notes that the foundation stone is referred to repeatedly as the Stone of Love.

In the address Rudolf Steiner gave after the foundation stone was placed in the soil, and the excavation covered up, he pointedly refers to the 'Fifth Gospel' – the additional descriptions of the life of Jesus Christ granted

---

[22] Lecture 5th June 1910 in GA 125.

to Rudolf Steiner and given to various groups of anthroposophists in the years 1913 and 1914. This leads one to conclude that this developing five-fold nature of humanity is paralleled by the four classical gospels which have now become five in number. In a similar way the four-fold human being is now on its way to a being a five-fold being, as the Spirit-Self develops; a process which itself has been so mightily assisted by anthroposophy.

Regarding the names of the hierarchies:
There are three lines in the verse where the names of the divine-hierarchical beings were spoken by Rudolf Steiner. However, these names are omitted in the published versions, and also here they are indicated by (…). The reason for indicating these names by dots is that Rudolf Steiner emphasized that these names are actually 'terms of power' and if in speaking this verse one includes these names, then a definite spiritual event occurs, invoking the influence of these beings into the speaker's soul.

This was in order for himself to do, since he was an initiate. But, as is reported in an addendum to the English edition of the Christmas Foundation Conference, he expressed his concern to Marie Steiner about the effect of these names being spoken by members, in society meetings. He had spoken the Greek of these names on this occasion, not the German formulations normally used.

The act of so invoking these divine beings does result in an effect, and the person so doing, has to be sure that they can sustain the effect of this. To deal with this situation, Rudolf Steiner coined a very general expression for the three groupings of spiritual beings, such as "You Spirits of Light". It is not fully clear unfortunately, from the remarks that have been handed down, as to whether this caution applies to reciting the verse before members, as well as to inwardly speaking these names in meditation. If the latter also applies, then it is important that the meditant is very clear about the implication of invoking the names.

It is to be regretted that this matter was not more fully elaborated for posterity. However, from other statements he made in the Esoteric School, it is seems clear that the meditant who feels that their own developing spirituality permits, may actually use these Greek names. He had stated to the members of that School, that the Greek names were to be used only in a serious, sincere context, as they were indeed 'words of power'.

Therefore I have used the bracketed dots to indicate that when the initiate spoken the verse, the hierarchical names were used. The earnest meditant can then use the names at that point, if that is one's decision. But they should not be used in reciting the verse in meetings.

THE FOUNDATION STONE MEDITATION

Human soul !
You live in the limbs
Which bear you through the world of Space
Into the ocean-being of the Spirit,
Practise Spirit-Remembering
In depths of soul,
Where in empowered efficacy
Of the cosmos Creator
Your own I comes into being
Within the I of God;
Then you truly will live
In the cosmic nature of the human being.

For efficacious is the Father-Spirit of the Heights,
Engendering Being in the depths of the cosmos:
You Spirits of the Forces !
(...   ...   ...)
Let from the Heights resound
What in the depths is echoed:
This is spoken:
Ex Deo Nascimur –
'From the Divine, humanity has its being.'
The Spirits hear this
 In east, west, north, south:
May human beings hear it !

Human Soul !
You live in the pulse of heart and lungs,
Which leads you through the rhythm of time
Into the sensing of your own soul's being;
Practise Spirit Contemplating
In equilibrium of soul,
Where the on surging
Deeds of cosmic evolving
Unite your own I
With the I of the Cosmos;
Then you truly will feel
In the dynamics of the human soul.

For efficacious is the Christ-will from horizon unto horizon,
Bestowing Grace on the soul within the rhythms of
                                        the cosmos
You Spirits of Light !
(... ... ...)
Let from the east be enkindled,
What through the west is formed.
This is spoken:
In Christo Morimur –
'In Christ, death becomes life.'
The Spirits hear this
In east, west, north, south:
May human beings hear it !

Human Soul !
You live in the resting head,
Which, from the foundations of Eternity
Discloses for you the Cosmic Thoughts:
Practise Spirit Beholding
In serenity of thought,
Where the eternal aims of the Gods
Bestow on your own I
The light of Cosmic Being
That the will may be free.
Then you truly will think
 In the foundations of the human spirit.

For efficacious are the Spirit's cosmic thoughts,
Invoking light into the being of the cosmos;
You Spirits of Soul !
(... ... ...)
Let from the depths be entreated,
What in the Heights shall be heard.
This is spoken:
Per Spiritum Sanctum Reviviscimus —
'In the cosmic thoughts of the Spirit the soul awakens.'
The Spirits hear this
In east, west, north, south:

May human beings hear it !
At the Turning-point of Time

The light of the Spirit of the Cosmos
Entered the earthly stream of being.
Darkness of night had lost its efficacy;
Day-radiant light streamed into human souls;
A Light,
That enwarms the simple shepherds' hearts,
A Light,
that enlightens the wise heads of kings.
Light Divine !
Christ-Sun !
Enwarm our hearts,
Enlighten our heads,
That good may come of
what in our hearts is laid down,
of what in our heads we resolve.

        Transl. Dr. Adrian Anderson

****

The Greek names indicated by dots:
In section A :Seraphim, Cherubim, Thronoi
In section B: Kyriotetes, Dynamis, Exusiai
In section C: Archai Archangeloi, Angeloi

There follows the same text, but with graphics, showing which sections are to be used on each day of the week.

How to use the seven sections for the weekly rhythm:

There are seven extracts, each consisting of two parts, which should be used following the rhythm of the week. The following diagram shows this; but at the end of this section the actual texts to be used for each day are written out. So on Monday for example, one meditates upon two specific extracts namely, "Light divine, Christ-Sun" <u>and</u> "The Spirits hear this in east, west, north, south, may human beings hear it !

One links these two separate statements together, three times, thus forming one potent meditative text. To help with the understanding of which two extracts are for which day, I have added the initials of the name of the days to the text above, as well as the broken lines to indicate exactly which section of the text is to be used on that day: e.g.

a5   su,we,fr,sa ⟶ **Practise Spirit-Remembering**
a6   **In depths of soul,**

This means that lines a5 and a6, are to be meditated upon on Sunday, Wednesday, Friday and Saturday, so this extract is used on several days; but on each day, it is used with another, a different extract. To find out what other extract is to be used with this on, say, Wednesday, just look down the section further – it is lines a9 & a10. Whereas on Fridays, it is a13 & a14. You can also look up the commentary on these lines under a5, a6.

THE FOUNDATION STONE MEDITATION
(With the sections to be used on each day shown)

a1	**Human soul !**
a2 tu	You live in the limbs
a3	Which bear you through the world of space
a4	Into the ocean-being of the Spirit,
a5 su,we,fr,sa	**Practise Spirit-Remembering**
a6	In depths of soul,
a7	Where in the empowered efficacy of
a8	the cosmos Creator
a9	Your own I comes into being
a10 we,th	Within the I of God;
a11	Then you truly will live
a12 th	In the cosmic nature of the human being.
a13 tu,fr	For efficacious is the Father-Spirit of the Heights,
a14	Engendering Being in the depths of the cosmos:
a15	You Spirits of the Forces:
a16 sa	Seraphim, cherubim, thrones !
a17	Let from the Heights resound
a18	What in the depths is echoed:
a19	This is heard:
a20	**Ex Deo Nascimur –**
a21	'From the Divine, humanity has its being.'
a22	The Spirits hear this
a23 mo	In East, West, North, South:
a24	May human beings hear it !
b1	**Human Soul !**
b2 tu	You live in the pulse of heart and lungs,
b3	Which leads you through the rhythm of time
b4	Into the sensing of your own soul's being;
b5 su,we,fr,sa	**Practise Spirit Contemplating**
b6	In equilibrium of soul,
b7	Where the on-surging
b8	Deeds of cosmic evolving
b9	Unite your own I
b10 we,th	With the I of the Cosmos;
b11	Then you truly will feel
b12 th	Within the dynamics of the human soul.

b13, tu, fr b14	For efficacious is the Christ-will from horizon unto horizon, bestowing Grace on the soul in the rhythms of the cosmos
b15 b16 sa b17 b18	You Spirits of Light ! (… … …) Let from the east be enkindled, What through the west is formed.
b19	This is spoken:
b20	**In Christo Morimur** –
b21	'In Christ, death becomes life.'
b22 b23 mo b24	The Spirits hear this In east, west, north, south: May human beings hear it !

c1 c2 tu	**Human Soul** ! You live in the resting head,
c3	Which, from the foundations of Eternity
c4	Discloses for you the Cosmic Thoughts:
c5 su,we, fr, sa c6	**Practise Spirit Beholding** In serenity of thought,
c7	Where the eternal aims of the Gods
c8 c9 we,th c10	Bestow on your own I The light of Cosmic Being That the will may be free.
c11 c12 th	Then you truly will think In the foundations of the human spirit.

c13 c14 tu, fr	For efficacious are the Spirit's cosmic thoughts, Invoking light into the being of the cosmos;
c15 c16 c17 sa c18	You Spirits of Soul ! (… … …) Let from the depths be entreated, What in the Heights shall be heard.
c19	This is spoken:
c20	**Per Spiritum Sanctum Reviviscimus**
c21	'In the cosmic thoughts of the Spirit the soul awakens.'
c22 c23 mo c24	The Spirits hear this In east, west, north, south: May human beings hear it !

d1	At the Turning-point of Time
d2	The light of the Spirit of the Cosmos
d3	Entered the earthly stream of being.
d4	Darkness of night had lost its efficacy;
d5	Day-radiant light streamed into human souls;
d6	A light,
d7	That enwarms the simple shepherds' hearts,
d8	A light,
d9	That enlightens the wise heads of kings.
d10	Light Divine,
d11 mo	Christ-Sun,
d12	Enwarm our hearts,
d13	Enlighten our heads,
d14	That good may come of
d15 su	what in our hearts is laid down,
d16	of what in our heads we resolve.

****

Following is a section where the actual parts of the verse to be used for each day are written out.

Sunday: {Human soul ! } practise Spirit-Remembering, practise Spirit-Contemplating, practise Spirit-Beholding – that good may come of what in our hearts is laid down, of what in our heads we resolve.

Monday: Light Divine, Christ-Sun – The Spirits hear this in east, west north, south: may human beings hear it ! (is repeated this three times)

Tuesday: { Human soul !} You live in the limbs…for efficacious is the Father-Spirit of the Heights, engendering Being in the depths of the cosmos // you live in the pulse of heart and lungs….for efficacious is the Christ-will from horizon unto horizon, bestowing Grace on the soul in the rhythms of the cosmos. // you live in the resting head…for efficacious are the Spirit's cosmic thoughts, invoking light into the being of the cosmos

Wednesday: practise Spirit-Remembering in depths of soul…your own I comes into being within the I of God // practise Spirit-Contemplating in equilibrium of soul…unite your own I with the I of the cosmos // practise Spirit-Beholding in serenity of thought…bestow on your own I the light of cosmic Being, that the will may be free.

Thursday: Your own I comes into being within the I of God; Then you truly will live in the cosmic nature of the human being // Unite your own I with the I of the Cosmos; then you truly will feel in the dynamics of the human soul // Bestow on your own I the light of Cosmic Being that the will may be free. Then you truly will think in the foundations of the human spirit.

Friday: Practise Spirit-Remembering in depths of soul…for efficacious is the Father-Spirit of the Heights, engendering Being in the depths of the cosmos // practise Spirit-Contemplating in equilibrium of soul…for efficacious is the Christ-will from horizon unto horizon, bestowing Grace on the soul in the rhythms of the cosmos // practise Spirit-Beholding in serenity of thought….for efficacious are the Spirit's cosmic thoughts, invoking light in the being of the cosmos

Saturday: Practise Spirit-Remembering in depths of soul….You Spirits of the Forces ! ( ), let from the Heights resound, what in the depths is echoed… / practise Spirit-Contemplating in equilibrium of soul…You Spirits of Light ! ( ), let from the east be enkindled what through the west is formed / Practise Spirit-Beholding in serenity of thought….You Spirits of Soul ! ( ), let from the depths be entreated, what in the Heights shall be heard.

5: THE PLACING OF THE FOUNDATION STONE OF THE GENERAL ANTHROPOSOPHICAL SOCIETY

It is necessary to comment on the translation. This text is perhaps the most difficult text in the entire corpus of transcripts from Rudolf Steiner's lectures. It is evident that he was speaking in an extraordinary circumstance, as the words do not separate into sentences, but flow on. It is as if the speaker receives inspirational ideas, and engages in the struggle to give expression to them, and their origin is so transcendental that they can hardly be expressed in human speech. Members of the audience could no doubt follow the train of thought being expressed, by intuitively knowing as listeners, where the phrases end and how these connect to the overall context.

Nevertheless there are awkward stylistic elements, which are quite foreign to Rudolf Steiner's normal, superb lecturing style. Hence when this text is presented in written form, its structure has to be altered. I have taken great care to ensure that precisely the same mental images which arise as one reads the German also arise from the English version. However, the text is still not a smoothly flowing text, as it retains the 'strained' nuance of the original. To remove this would be to re-cast the text into a different literary genre, and to fail to present the remarkable ambience of the occasion.

****

Address by Rudolf Steiner on 25th December 1923, at 10 am
(Dr. Steiner greeted those present with the words:)

My dear friends, as the first words today, there should resound through our hall the summary of that which can stand before your souls as the most important result of the previous year.

After this some comments will be made about these summarizing words. But first let our ears hear these words, in order to renew according to our understanding, from the signs of the present times, the old maxim of the Mysteries, "know yourself",

(Part of the Foundation Stone verse is then spoken: sections a,b, c.).

Human soul !
You live in the limbs
Which bear you through the world of Space
Into the ocean-being of the Spirit,
Practise Spirit-Remembering
In depths of soul,
Where in the empowered efficacy
Of the cosmos Creator
Your own I comes into being
Within the I of God;
Then you truly will live
In the cosmic-nature of the human being.

For efficacious is the Father-Spirit of the Heights,
Engendering Being in depths of the cosmos:
Let from the Heights resound
What in the depths is echoed:
This is spoken:
Ex Deo Nascimur –

'From the Divine, humanity has its being.'
The Spirits hear this
In east, west, north, south:
May human beings hear it !

Human Soul !
You live in the pulse of heart and lungs,
Which leads you through the rhythm of time
Into the sensing of your own soul's being;
Practise Spirit Contemplating
In equilibrium of soul,
Where the on surging
Deeds of cosmic evolving
Unite your own I
With the I of the Cosmos;
Then you truly will feel
In the dynamics of the human soul.

For efficacious is the Christ-will from horizon unto horizon,
bestowing Grace on the soul within the rhythms of the cosmos
Let from the east be enkindled,
What through the west is formed.
This is spoken:
In Christo Morimur –
'In Christ, death becomes life.'
The Spirits hear this
In east, west, north, south:
May human beings hear it !

Human Soul !
You live in the resting head,
Which, from the foundations of Eternity
Discloses for you the Cosmic Thoughts:
Practise Spirit Beholding
In serenity of thought,
Where the eternal aims of the Gods
Bestow on your own I
The light of Cosmic Being
That the will may be free.
Then you truly will think
In the foundations of the human spirit.

For efficacious are the Spirit's cosmic thoughts,
Invoking light into the being of the cosmos;
Let from the depths be entreated,

What in the Heights shall be heard.
This is spoken:
Per Spiritum Sanctum Reviviscimus -
"In the cosmic thoughts of the Spirit the soul awakens.'
The Spirits hear this
In east, west, north, south:
May human beings hear it !

My dear friends! When today I look back specifically to that which was able to be obtained from the spiritual worlds, whilst terrible storms of war surged through the world, it must be summarized in the form of a threefold verse, which has just resounded in your ears.

It was possible to perceive {during this time} that particular threefold nature of the human being, through which the human being, in its entirety of spirit, soul and body, is able to endow with life in a new way, that ancient maxim, "know yourself". For decades this threefold membering[23] could be perceived. I myself was not able to bring this perception to maturity until the previous decade, a time when the storms of war were raging.

At that time I attempted to indicate how the human being lives physically in its metabolic-limb system, in its heart-rhythmical system, in its head-thinking and perception system. From knowledge of the threefold nature of the human being, one can be convinced of significant matters, but one must take up into oneself this threefold structuring in the right way. This right way is by the enlivening of the heart with Anthroposophia, as I

---

[23] the old English verb , 'to member' , that is, to is integrate a part into the larger whole, is exactly the meaning needed here

indicated yesterday. (See appendix 1 for the remarks referred to here.)

The significant matter is this; in the first instance the human being, from this knowledge of the threefold nature of humanity, recognizes something important. Firstly, it becomes clear that he cognizes through his feelings and his will. From this process he recognizes what it is that he actually does when – enlivened by cosmic spirits – he places himself in the world of space through his limbs.

What is it that the human being then recognizes? Through fulfilling his duties, his mission and his obligations in the world, and in a really active comprehension of the world, the human being recognizes the nature of human and cosmic Love, which as a part of the universe, is manifesting its efficacy throughout creation.

But also significant is the wonderful secret that prevails between lungs and heart, in which cosmic rhythms are expressed, inwardly perceptible. There it is brought to expression how cosmic rhythms – active throughout millennia, throughout aeons – beat in the rhythm of our pulse and blood, bringing about a cosmic en-souling within the human being.

One can hope, indeed be quite convinced, that this wonderful secret will be understood wisely, with the heart as the organ of cognition. In this way, the human being can experience how cosmic images – those God-given images[24] – so actively bring the cosmos into manifestation from themselves.[25]

---

[24] This phrase could lead to confusion, because he is speaking here of the 3rd person of the Trinity, the Holy Spirit, and the divine beings in

Just as in actively moving oneself, one is taking hold of the efficacious cosmic Love,[26] so too, one will (eventually) take hold of the archetypes of cosmic being. This will occur when one feels in oneself the mysterious transition between the rhythm of the cosmos and the rhythm of the heart. And also when through this process one feels the human rhythm which mysteriously plays between the lungs and the heart.

The human being could take hold of the archetypes of cosmic existence through sensing with his feelings, in the right way, what reveals itself in his head system, which is quiescent upon his shoulders,[27] even when he is walking. If the human being does this, then – feeling himself in his head-system – and with the warmth of the heart pouring itself into this head-system – he will experience in his own being the presence of efficacious, interweaving cosmic thoughts.

---

who interweave the cosmic Imaginations (divine thought-forms) from Creation is fashioned. However, R. Steiner emphasizes that such Imaginations ultimately derive from God, the First Person of the Trinity; "What the philosophers call the Absolute, the 'eternal being', the foundational element of the cosmos, what the religions call God, we call the Idea." (*Goethe's Natural Scientific Writings*, p. 162, German edition (GA. 1)

[25] This phrase refers to the cosmic imaginative thoughts of the divine beings which serve as a guide and catalyst for the gods, and lesser beings who serve them, to create and sustain the cosmos.

[26] This phrase means that, unknown to our conscious mind, the actual power underlying our will, such as its resolution that we shall walk or move our arms, derives from divine Will, which is itself, Love.

[27] Here emphasis is being put upon the phenomenological approach to the body, in order to see its relevance to the soul quality with which it is associated. The head needs motionlessness, just as the thinker needs to be motionless for intense thinking.

And in this way he will become the trinity of all being; cosmic Love, efficacious within human love[28]; cosmic imagination, efficacious in the corporeal structuring of the human being; and cosmic thoughts, mysteriously active like a substratum within human thoughts.

The human being will comprehend this threefold nature and recognize himself as an individual, independent person within the cosmic efficacy of the gods. The human being will comprehend himself as a cosmic human being, as an individual person within the cosmic being; and will understand himself to be efficacious for the future of the cosmos – as an individual person within the cosmic human being.[29] The human being will renew the old maxim, 'Know yourself' from the signs of the present times.

The ancient Greeks could still omit an additional phrase, namely "of spirit, soul and body", because with them the human self had not yet become so abstract as it is with us. With us it has merged into the abstract ego-point, or at the most, into thinking, feeling and willing. But with the Greeks, human nature was understood as an entirety, consisting of spirit, soul and body. Thus the Greeks could believe that they were considering the entire human being of spirit, soul and body, when they allowed that ancient

---

[28] The same German term, 'waltend' which I have dealt with earlier, regarding the fact the God is not all-mighty, occurs here, and again one sees that 'efficacious' — having a definite, active influence — is meant, not 'ruling/reigning/all-wielding, for such autocratic or power-based dynamics are alien to divine Love. The same holds true for the this word in ref. 26

[29] The German can be rendered as the cosmic human being, or cosmic human nature; it refers to the macrocosmic or archetypal spiritual reality of the human being; in particular our threefold spirit, which has its existence in the zodiacal cosmos.

maxim, that primordial Sun-word, the Apollo word, "Know thyself!" to resound.

But we have to say, when we renew this maxim from reading the signs of the times in the right way, "O human soul, know yourself, in your living interweaving, in spirit, soul and body." Then we will have understood that which is the foundation of all human beings. Then we will have understood this cosmic substance in which these three spiritual realities are having a living efficacious existence:

The Spirit which streams from the heights, and manifests itself in the human head;

The Christ-power which is efficacious throughout the periphery of the horizon, which weaves in and through the streams of air, circling around the Earth, and which actively has an influence within our breathing system;
and thirdly, forces rising up from the interior of the Earth, which are active in our limbs.

We need to unite these three forces – the forces of the heights, forces of the horizon's periphery and the forces of the depths – and in that moment we unite these three into one forming substance. Then having done that, our soul, in its comprehension of this process, can compare the human dodecahedron with the cosmic dodecahedron.[30]

---

[30] This sentence appears to indicate that we can best contemplate the central dynamic of the entire verse – the creation and subsequent emergence of the human 'life-wave' from its creators within the 12-fold zodiac cosmos – once we have gained some awareness of, and been able in some way, to respond to the efficacy of the Trinity, the triune Godhead.

From these three forces; from the spirit of the Heights, from the Christ-power of the horizon's periphery, from the efficacy of the Father, the Creator-Father activity, which streams up from the depths, we now want to form in our souls in this moment, the dodecahedral foundation stone. This stone: we place into the substratum of our souls,[31] in order that there it can become a powerful sign within the strong foundations of our soul-existence, and that throughout the future activity of the Anthroposophical Society, we may stand upon this firm foundation stone.

We want to remain forever conscious of this foundation stone, formed today for the Anthroposophical Society. We want to remember always this foundation stone, which today we have placed in the depths of our hearts, during everything that we will to do in supporting, developing, and in bringing to full unfolding the Anthroposophical Society. The threefold human being teaches us of {cosmic} Love, of cosmic Imagination, of cosmic Thoughts.

Let us seek in him the substance of cosmic Love, which we have established as our foundation. Let us seek in the human being the archetype of the Imagination in accordance with which we are forming cosmic Love in our hearts. And let us seek the power of thought from the heights, so that we can let this imaginative dodecahedral creation, formed of Love, become appropriately radiant !

Then we shall carry away with us from here that which we need; for then the foundation stone will shine

---

[31] Notice how this expression mirrors the sentence in the 1913 ritual speech; "this stone, the symbol of our soul, will be placed down into the densified realm of the elements".

brightly. That foundation stone which has its *substance* from cosmic-human Love, its *graphically vivid quality*, its *form*, from cosmic-human Imagination, and that *radiant light* from cosmic-human thoughts. That radiant light which, when we remember this moment, can always shine towards us, with a warm light that also arouses our action, our thinking, our feeling and our willing.

And what is the right soil in which we must place today's foundation stone ? That right soil is our hearts in their harmonious co-operation. In their good will, a will permeated with love, which wants to work together to carry the anthroposophical Will through the world. And this Will shall be able to ray out towards us, like an exhortation, from the thought-radiance[32] that at all times can shine towards us from the dodecahedral stone of Love, which we today want to place deep in our hearts.

This, my dear friends, we want to take up into our souls in the truest and best way, and thereby we want to en-warm our souls, and thereby we want to illumine our souls. And we want to preserve this soul-warmth and this soul-light, which today we have planted by our good will into our hearts. We are planting this, my dear friends, in a moment when human remembrance, which truly understands the world, looks back to that point in humanity's development which was the Turning Point of Time.

That moment when from the darkness of night, and from the darkness of the moral feeling of humanity, that divine being was born who became the Christ, the Spiritual

---

[32] This expression refers to the powerful radiance that the formative cosmos-sustaining 'thought-forms' of the Gods inherently possess.

Being who came to dwell in humanity; striking in like light from heaven.[33]

We are best able to empower this soul-warmth and soul-light, which we need, if we enliven it with that warmth and that light which rayed in as the Christ-Light at the turning point of time in the darkness of the world.

And we want to enkindle the primal Christmas night, which occurred two thousand years ago, in our hearts, in our minds, in our will, so that it may help us when we seek to carry out into the world that which shines towards us from that thought-radiance of the dodecahedral Love-Foundation-Stone.

That foundation stone which is modelled from the cosmos and then placed in the human being. Thus may our heart's feeling be turned towards the primal Christmas in old Palestine.

(The last section only of the Foundation Stone verse, section d, is then spoken.)

At the Turning-point of Time
The light of the Spirit of the Cosmos
Entered the earthly stream of being.
Darkness of night had lost its efficacy;
Day-radiant light streamed into human souls;
A Light,
That enwarms the simple shepherds' hearts,
A Light,
that enlightens the wise heads of kings.

---

[33] This integration of looking back to the event of Golgotha, in the ceremony, also occurred just after the 1913 ceremony, when the sublime macrocosmic Lord's prayer was spoken and commented on. In 1923, the lecture cycle on World History was given.

Light Divine !
Christ-Sun !
Enwarm our hearts,
Enlighten our heads,
That good may come of
what in our hearts is laid down,
of what we in our heads resolve.

This feeling that reaches back to the primal Christmas can give to us the power to enwarm our hearts, to illumine our heads, which we need in order to practise in the right way – anthroposophically efficacious – that which can arise from the threefold knowledge of humanity, a knowledge which harmonizes itself into a unity.

Therefore – bringing together what we have been contemplating here – let there once again be placed before our souls, that which arises out of a real understanding of the maxim, "Know yourself according to body, soul and spirit." Let this now be set before us with the same efficacy that it manifests in the cosmos.[34]

In this way to our stone which we have placed deep in our hearts, and thus also to human life and human existence and human activity, there may speak that which the world everywhere has to proclaim to human existence and human life and human activity.
(The Foundation Stone verse – sections a, b, c – is then spoken.)

Human soul !

---

[34] This phrase is indicating that the great verse, which is about to be recited, should now be so experienced, that it has a formative effect upon the listeners, similar to the effect which the 'cosmic word' has upon humanity — i.e., that 'word' which is made manifest through the 12-fold zodiac, but originating from the Trinity.

You live in the limbs
Which bear you through the world of Space
Into the ocean-being of the Spirit,
Practise Spirit-Remembering
In depths of soul,
Where in the empowered efficacy
Of the cosmos Creator
Your own I comes into being
Within the I of God;
Then you truly will live
In the cosmic-nature of the human being.

For efficacious is the Father-Spirit of the Heights,
Engendering Being in depths of the cosmos:
Let from the Heights resound
What in the depths is echoed:
This is spoken:
Ex Deo Nascimur –
'From the Divine humanity has its being.'
The Spirits hear this
In east, west, north, south:
May human beings hear it !

Human Soul !
You live in the pulse of heart and lungs,
Which leads you through the rhythm of time
Into the sensing of your own soul's being;
Practise Spirit Contemplating
In equilibrium of soul,
where the on-surging
Deeds of cosmic evolving
Unite your own I
With the I of the Cosmos;
Then you truly will feel
In the dynamics of the human soul.

For efficacious is the Christ-will from horizon unto
                                                  horizon,
Bestowing Grace on the soul within the rhythms of
the cosmos.

Let from the east be enkindled,
What through the west is formed.
This is spoken:
In Christo Morimur –
'In Christ, death becomes life.'
The Spirits hear this
In east, west, north, south:
May human beings hear it !

Human Soul !
You live in the resting head,
Which, from the foundations of Eternity
Discloses for you the Cosmic Thoughts:
Practise Spirit Beholding
In serenity of thought,
Where the eternal aims of the Gods
Bestow on your own I
The light of Cosmic Being
That the will may be free.
Then you truly will think
In the foundations of the human spirit.
For efficacious are the Spirit's cosmic thoughts,
Invoking light into the being of the cosmos.
Let from the depths be entreated,
What in the Heights shall be heard.

This is spoken:
Per Spiritum Sanctum Reviviscimus
'In the cosmic thoughts of the Spirit the soul awakens.'

The Spirits hear this
In east, west, north, south:
May human beings hear it !

****

Appendix A

From the address given by Rudolf Steiner on the 24th December 1923.

... now the *spiritual* content of the anthroposophical movement can appear, like *constructive* flames for our hearts, not like destructive flames {that burnt down our building}. For in all sorts of ways, warmth can speak to us from the spiritual content of the anthroposophical movement. Warmth, which can be able to enliven countless seeds for the spiritual life of the future, which is contained precisely in the soil of Dornach and all that belongs to it.

...I have appealed to your hearts, to that aspect of your wisdom which through your hearts is aglow, and through your hearts can become aglow with enthusiasm.

6   Commentary on the Foundation Stone verse

The verse has four sections; section A is concerned with the will, (reflected in the limbs) and also with the first of the Trinity, Father-God. It is also concerned with Intuition or the highest of our three spiritual faculties. Section B is concerned with the emotional capacities and sensitivity to sensory perception, these are reflected in the heart and lungs, and it is also concerned with the second of the Trinity, the Son, or Logos of St. John's gospel. Therefore section B is also concerned with the faculty of Inspiration, which I have termed *Cosmic-Spiritual Consciousness* in *The Way to the Sacred.*

Section C is about thinking, physiologically reflected in the head, and it also concerns the third member of the Trinity, the Holy Spirit. Consequently it is about the faculty of Imagination, or what I term *Psychic-Image Awareness*. Section D is about the coming to Earth of the Christ and the implications of this. It is important to bear in mind that Section A is more difficult to understand than section B and certainly section C, because it is an exploration of the dynamics involved, in developing *Intuition* or what I call *High Initiation Consciousness* in my book, The Way to the Sacred.

Section A

a1 **Human soul !**
The usual translation is, Soul of Man. This is only apparently sexist as Rudolf Steiner used a non-gender specific German term. The lack of non-sexist term in English for human being is a problem here.

a4 **Into the ocean-being of the Spirit**

This can also grammatically be: in the ocean-being of the Spirit. This nuance implies a time-transcending dynamic of humanity, especially in our volitional life; namely that in our wills we are in effect, already in the ocean-being of the spiritual worlds. In so far as our limbs are an expression of our will, and are an expression in matter of it, we are already in the spirit – but unconsciously. However, the nuance of, "in the ocean-being of the Spirit" may also refer to deeds intuitively carried out which have a direct connection the higher spiritual worlds. In that sense one is already in the spirit, however still not fully consciously.

a5 Practise Spirit-Remembering

It is vital that one understands the meaning of "Spirit-Remembering". The special meaning of 'remembering' is indicated by the way Rudolf Steiner himself used it, as recorded in his lecture transcripts. Since it associated with the highest of the three states of spiritual awareness, it is also the most difficult to understand.

To practise *remembering* — as is required for the Evening Review exercise — means that one consciously scrutinizes one's inner life (especially the will-impulses). As the initiate explained, "to *remember* is to consciously gaze within oneself….remembering is truly a deepened, empowered day-consciousness" (28/Aug/1915). These words define clearly the inner dynamics that are involved when one reviews the day, that is, one inwardly re-capitulates one's deeds.

This is clearly a re-incorporating (i.e., literally re-member-ing) the past actions into one's consciousness and life. It is a searching to perceive qualities in one's own volition, *and then trying to sense the spiritual realities pulsing within it.* Therefore the term 'remembering' (erinnern) has a root meaning here, similar to what 're-member' originally meant in English, that is, to re-incorporate. Now, the soul exercise of Spirit-Remembering is similar to the Evening Review. Indeed it actually merges into it when this review is given an esoteric extension – by including the prior evening's night-time experiences, primarily one's dreams. (This activity is explained in detail in *The Way to the Sacred*.) This extended review process was recommended by Rudolf Steiner to those on the path to self-initiation. So an excellent way towards the practise of Spirit-Remembrance is the extended Evening Review.

In a lecture of 1907 (4th Feb) the initiate explains that the above activity – of consciously gazing within oneself – has the implication that one invokes within oneself a "shadowy echo" of <u>that which flows from the Father God</u>, or First Logos into our spiritual depths. "When you contemplate your own will-forces, that which in you is able to **will**, then you have a shadowy echo of that which flows from the power of the Atma, from the Godhead."

This throws much light on the remarkable text in lines a9 and 10. But to fully carry out Spirit-Remembrance encompasses a much more demanding activity than the Evening Review, namely the activity described by Rudolf Steiner in *Knowledge of Higher Worlds* and elsewhere, with regard to attaining to *Intuition*.

Meditation actually consists of three phases of different inner activity. The phases and the threshold experiences they bring are described in *The Way to the Sacred*. There is firstly the focussing on a verse, allowing 'holistic' insights to occur (the spiritual truths or 'ideas' clothed by the verse, which exist in the astral sphere, and which light up within one's ether body). Then the second phase involves focussing on the spiritual forces involved in such an inner activity.

This second mode of meditating is designated as Contemplation by Rudolf Steiner. After ending this second process, one then attempts to remain conscious of spiritual intuitions, but now without any tangible focus of one' efforts; that is, the mind is not focussed on any definable subject. This third phase was not designated by a specific name but is that process which leads to the third, the highest state of initiatory consciousness, Intuition, the faculty which is the herald of our highest spiritual element, the Spirit-Man or Spirit-Human.

Meditation on this part of the Foundation Stone verse gradually discloses profound insights into this Spirit-Man or Atma element of our spiritual nature. The advanced meditant can gradually become aware of the divine source of our will-forces, once the practise of Spirit-Remembering deepens into the third phase of meditating. Our will forces derive from God, formed through the efficacy of the First Hierarchy, which is in turn assisted by the Principalities, their reflection in the lower spheres of divine beings. See the commentary to lines, a9, a10 for further indications about this.

The term, 'Spirit' in this line, and for all three sections (a5, b5, c5), is deliberately ambiguous. It refers therefore to both the spiritual reality <u>beyond</u> the human being, and the spiritual reality <u>within</u> the meditant. So, one is called upon to re-capitulate inwardly one's actions and in this way to become more enlightened regarding the spiritual reality in one's own volition, and the connection of this to the spiritual beings from whom our Will derives.

Naturally the expectation here is to only make a start towards the extraordinary, lofty state of being fully conscious in the Will. For this state is not just a sensing, but a direct perception of the unity of one's inner being to the origin of our will forces – our Creator – and hence this state therefore bestows consciousness of the heights of the Spiritual Worlds. When fully attained, it gives eternality of ego-consciousness, invoking a consciousness that merges with the Higher Self in which is awareness of all of one's past lives.

a7 **Where**

The term 'where' has various meanings here, and in the parallel lines in sections B and C. Firstly, it indicates that, through this exercise, the meditant is approaching near to the activity that is being undertaken by the member of the Trinity (or hierarchical beings associated with it). These processes are, in section A: 'comes into being', in B; 'unites with' and in C: bestows 'cosmic-light'. Secondly, it means as the inner exercise is being undertaken within the meditant, spiritual powers are more able to carry out the specific deed within her or him.

A7....**the empowered efficacy**

Whereas in lines a,b,c13, deity is described as 'efficacious', for reasons which I gave in detail earlier, here in a7, the activity of Deity here is more accomplishing, less subject to opposition. Because here the implication is that at this third or highest state of initiatory consciousness, the meditant encounters and merges with divine reality, and at that level, where creation is being brought into existence. Hence the efficacy, whilst still not reigning absolutely, is more empowered.

a9, a10 **own I, the I of God**

The German term here should be translated as "I", not 'self 'or 'ego'. The word, 'ego' is incorrect here, it is an <u>external</u> psychological designation of personal selfhood (with overtones of psychoanalysis or such). Whereas the original German term, "Ich", means "I", the name we ourselves give to our inner being. However, the occurrence of the word "I" is a peculiar construction here, which may at first hinder the understanding of this verse.

It is precisely the peculiar nuance that is created by using the word, "I", which gives these two lines their efficacy when they are used in meditation. For with this word, "I", a human being designates their own innermost being, it directly expresses an existential perception of oneself. Similarly, the same word used of God, has to imply that aspect of the consciousness of God wherein the core of His self-awareness is found. To say that one's own "I" comes into being within the "I" of God, has the same meaning as declaring that "one's own Self comes into being within the Self of God", but the former version declares this meaning in a very different way.

The difference is that as soon as reference is made to one's own "I" arising into being, the word "I" immediately takes one into that self-consciousness or awareness of selfhood that we adults have. This little word takes us inside the core of our selfhood, which is precisely where the process is occurring at that moment. Whereas if the verse says 'self', then that is the same fact, but now we only encounter it from outside.

When we hear or read the word 'Self', we are simply made aware logically of a process which is said to be happening within us. When the word, "I", is used, however, the meditant has an existential experience of their selfhood, and what is happening to it. When hearing the phrase, *"unite your own ...* one is aware that a narrator is stating an idea to one. But as soon as the word "I" resonates inside one by really clearly, strongly experiencing it, (whether silently as in meditation, or in recitation) then the narrator of the verse merges with yourself. The result of this is that one is actually naming oneself, thus living inside one's own awareness of self.

This is a much more profound experience than if one uses the word, 'Self'. This immediately direct, intimate quality is strengthened by the use of the same linguistic approach in the last phrase, 'the I of God'. For then in this second line, the meditant is made aware not only of her or his own inner reality, but is also pointed towards, in some way, God's self-awareness, or experience of Himself.

Now, there is another very important point here, about which I would also like to give some seed-thoughts. The actual nature of God is a question that has to arise here. The commentary for line D2 (Spirit of the Cosmos) gives some pivotal perspectives on the nature of God, in the sense of that creator-being who is above the nine hierarchies. However, here a different aspect of this enigma needs to be considered.

The very idea of contemplating the "self" of God, or what He experiences in the equivalent of "I", may appear invalid, as God is so sublime. However, just as there are various aspects of the cosmic Christ in the teachings of Rudolf Steiner, so too of God. The Father-God has a reflection so to speak, in the lowest group of hierarchical beings, the third. This is with the Principalities, and in fact, with the most evolved of the Principalities.[35]

---

[35] R. Steiner, *Theosophy of the Rosicrucians*, lect. 9.

If one recalls that in antiquity, with unevolved souls, powerful elementals or tribal spirits are referred to as God, then the foremost of the 'Archai' is actually quite a lofty step in defining deity. But the Father-God is also reflected in the Thrones, from whom the Spirit-human emanated forth, in the remote Saturn Aeon.

One needs to bear in mind too, that all ranks of beings are evolving gradually, through an Aeon (the largest evolutionary phase). They move up to a higher rank, and thereby acquire a new, higher member, and also lose the lowest one. Illustration 4 shows precisely the elements or states of being that the Hierarchies possess (see end page).

Of course, God as the creator of the cosmos is actually of the ineffable Trinity which is above the Hierarchies, but He is reflected within the Thrones and the Principalities. These deities have been instrumental in creating our physical body, and our sense of 'I' as Spirit-human. Through this, we are able to experience selfhood.

The Principalities have a major influence in our development of selfhood, or the "I". The spiritual forces underlying our physical body is interwoven with the faculty of Atma or Spirit-human; the Spirit-human is the highest aspect of our true, eternal Self.

Our everyday "I" is balanced exactly between these two members of our being. Thus the Principalities are involved with both our everyday 'I' and also our higher 'I'. Illustration Four shows the profoundly significant fact that the Atma stage is the normal or 'ego' stage of the Principalities, and their lowest stage, out of which they are gradually growing, is the (equivalent of) what for us is everyday self-hood.

The "I" of the human being is then, in the first instance, as a reality nurtured within the Principalities, the fully conscious, empowered Atma stage, precisely that stage to which Section A of the great verse is referring. Namely that stage which human souls achieve through *Intuition*, and for which the practise of Spirit-Remembering is so important. This stage could be designated as the (true) Self or higher I of humanity.

The Principalities are living existentially within this 'Atma' stage, and the Thrones are the reflection of the Father-God in the First Hierarchy; so section A indicates that these deities are the link between us, our Spirit-human, and the primal Godhead. In early lectures the Father-God is referred to by Rudolf Steiner as reflected in the foremost of the Principalities, but in later lectures, it is the highest of the Thrones who is the defined in this way.

Furthermore, as Illustration Four shows, the highest level of being of the Principalities is called the "Father" stage, and this same level is the lowest element of the sublime Seraphim. The profound depths of this verse is also seen when one meditates on the fact that towards the end of the Saturn Aeon (also called Old Saturn), the Principalities were 'growing out of' their ego-hood, whilst the Seraphim's highest 'member' was the "Father" state. Thus our "I" is interlinked with God, through the various Hierarchical beings.

a12 In the cosmic nature of the human being

This line is poetically translatable as, 'In the cosmic being of Man', without any sexist inference being intended, the term 'Man' meaning the human being. Such expressions as the "All-Worlds-being of Man" are awkward and may obscure the meaning here, namely that the Spirit-Man, or Atma principle of humanity, has a cosmic existence. Attainment of union with this aspect of our spirit grants to the meditant a conscious functioning within the cosmic Spirit-Man state of being. Here as in b12 and c12, the paradox is taught that attainment of these initiatory states of cosmic consciousness takes one into the true human state.

a13 **Father-Spirit**

For those who find the apparently sexist nature of the expression 'Father-Spirit' disagreeable, it is important to note that the high degree initiation wisdom flowing through Rudolf Steiner is not at all sexist. The reason for this expression being formulated as masculine by him, and by earlier initiates, has to do with quite specific transcendental experiences concerning the nature of God, the Creator-Spirit.

This Creator becomes experienced by the initiate as carrying out actions which have qualities similar to the human volitional forces, or power of Will which was traditionally associated with men rather than with women. The activity is direct and powerful, and brings new life or projects into being.

Rudolf Steiner also pointed out that in earlier ages it was the case that men had a stronger natural connection to an externalized willing, whereas women had (and have) a natural connection to the nurturing, sustaining dynamics of the heart, whose capacity for loving kindness is associated with the Holy Spirit. Hence the Will-empowered divinity called 'God' was regarded as masculine, and the nurturing spiritual energies of the Spirit which bestows holiness, caused it to be regarded as feminine. Naturally wherever males dominated improperly over the women in general society, the masculinity of God would be emphasized in a false way, and the feminine dynamics of experiencing of wisdom were denied.

In modern times, both sexes should strive for a balanced relationship to these dynamics; and today such a division of the genders is questionable. The term in line a8, 'cosmos Creator' could have been used here, but Rudolf Steiner wishes to also indicate a kind of world-cross, i.e. forces from the heights (e.g., zodiac) interacting with a response from the depths (human volitional impulses in the material world), and also horizontal forces from the east and the west.

a14 **in the depths of the cosmos**
I have concluded that the phrase, 'in the depths of the cosmos' is the most appropriate for an ambiguous German expression. This verse, as with all deeper meditative verses, through the deliberate use of inclusive language, prompts one to be open to various associated meanings. It could also be rendered, 'in the depths of the worlds'.

The primary meaning of this line is explained in the address given when the verse was first spoken. The context here is of forces from God, having permeated inside our planet, rising up into the human being, into the will of human nature, and thus are also active within the body's limbs. For the limbs are the organs of our will.

However, since in line a8, deity is described as the 'Creator of the Cosmos' (that is, of multiple worlds, as the German means literally 'Worlds-Creator') this Being's activity of "engendering being" need not be thought of as restricted only to this planet. The word, 'engendering' may be queried, but this is the best way to render a term ('erzeugend') which in the original deliberately has procreative and Biblical nuances; a direct equivalent in English would be 'begetting'.

a20 **Ex Deo Nascimur**
This Latin phrase, like the two following in parts B and C, derives from the medieval founder of the Rosicrucian stream, Christian Rosenkreutz. It means literally, 'from God we are born'.

a21 **From the Divine, humanity has its being**
This line, as with the two Latin phrases in B and C, is followed by an 'interpreted translation' by Rudolf Steiner, which is provided in order to emphasize a particular nuance of meaning in it. If you find the term 'Divine' archaic, then of course be free to substitute another term, but bear in mind that Steiner uses a term ('dem Göttlichen') which is more inclusive than the being of 'God', thought of as a specific, separate Being.

So he is wanting to convey that our origin is from God in conjunction with other spiritual Beings — namely hierarchical Beings serving His Will. Hence you could substitute perhaps such expressions as, 'humanity is in the realms of God created' or, 'from realms of God does humanity arise'.

a22/23 **The spirits hear this in east, west, north, south**
The reference to the four directions is a phrase used by Rudolf Steiner to indicate that the <u>ethereal</u> cosmos, the universe on an etheric level.[36] The spiritual beings which are indicated here include the "Beings of the Elements" as well as the nature spirits with which we have some acquaintance. The former are not the simple elemental

---

[36] In a lect. Of 13.Nov 1921, in GA 208, p. 199.

beings or nature-spirits as such, they are the regents, the rulers, of these beings. In one version of the text of the verse, Rudolf Steiner wrote 'elemental beings', in another version, 'the spirits of the elements'.

a24 **May human beings hear it !**

The divine reality now present in the Earth's aura, will eventually be inwardly heard, not only seen as a new clairvoyance slowly develops. In Goethe's Faust, Act 1, Part 2, in Ariel's song, this aural sensitivity is described. Rudolf Steiner explains that it is precisely the spiritual realities within the Spiritual Sun-radiance which is absorbed by the finest of the ethers, the life-ether.

By gaining perception of the ether, the meditant can attain awareness, albeit indirect, of the higher spiritual solar reality. He taught that this has been done for millennia by students of the initiates, and this verse is suggesting that the students of the new Mysteries can attain this faculty, too.[37]

The composer Mendelssohn is an historical example of this. He had perception of the ethereal-astral realms. One exquisite composition of his derives, according to Rudolf Steiner, from what he so heard in a mystery centre near Iona in Scotland.[38] Here is an indication of that well-known revelation of Rudolf Steiner to Friedrich Rittelmeyer, that the way to the cosmic Christ is via

---

[37] The Gospel of St. Matthew lecture cycle; lect. 3

[38] R. Steiner in a lect. of 3/3/'11 taught that this composer's "Fingal's Cave" overture derives from his perception of an after-echo in the ethers in the cave of the Island of Staffa. This is where ancient Celtic mysteries carried out a water-initiation. The beautiful melody is strikingly evocative of the dynamics involved in the appearing and then disappearing of an ethereal water-elemental to consciousness.

striving to sense the spiritual beings in the seasons, and especially the role of the Christ in each season, influencing the elementals of each hemisphere, via an archangel. See this author's *Living a Spiritual Year* for an elucidation of the actual nature Rudolf Steiner's research on this subject.[39]

SECTION B

This is an exploration of the dynamics involved, both in oneself and in the spiritual realms, in developing *Inspiration* or Cosmic - *Spiritual Consciousness*, that is the second of the three states of initiate consciousness.

b5 Spirit-Contemplation

The term German, 'besinnen' has caused some confusion. Its actual meaning here is discovered in texts where he is explaining the nature of meditation. It is correctly translated as 'contemplation', as Contemplation (besinnen) is used by Rudolf Steiner technically to refer to an inner activity which occurs as the second stage of the meditation process. It is an inner sensing activity, different from normal meditation, which occurs after the specific focusing on a verse has finished.

One attempts then to enter into a silence, an inner quietness which becomes deeper and deeper. Then the actual spiritual dynamics, (active within one's astral body, but deriving from Life-spirit forces) that *have made possible* the meditative focus on an "imagination" – a text or symbol used in meditating – can be experienced.

---

[39] Adrian Anderson, *Living a Spiritual Year – seasonal festivals in northern and southern hemispheres*, Anthroposophic Press 1992, and Threshold Publishing 1992.

In striving to attain to that experience, one is developing the faculty of *Spiritual Consciousness* or *Inspiration*.

It is precisely this activity which is meant here, meditative activity is to be widened to include this second phase. However the implication of section B is that it should be practised in circumstances not restricted to one's meditation times. Contemplation is also practised, in a somewhat different mode, when one strives to sense the inner spiritual dynamics of the seasons of the year, or other natural rhythmical cycles.

The book, "Living a Spiritual Year" provides a description of these, and also stimulates the reader's own insights into these rhythms. Such activity is excellently assisted by the Soul Calendar – so long as one starts with the right date, which is based on the "Easter" date" of one's hemisphere (i.e., the first Sunday after the first full Moon after the spring equinox). The purpose of the Soul Calendar is to stimulate the faculty of Inspiration or *Spiritual Consciousness* by developing this sensitivity to the rhythms of the year, of the seasons, of the week.

b10 The I of the Cosmos (das Welten-Ich)

Rudolf Steiner uses this term 'das Welten-Ich' to refer to two distinct beings. Firstly, the Son or Logos (2nd of the Trinity also known as the 3 Logoi), secondly, the highest of the Sun-spirits. The primary meaning of this expression is the zodiacal Logos, which is the same as the classical World-Soul of antiquity. The concept of the Logos or Word in anthroposophy, as in St. John's gospel, is that sublime being who is responsible for the coming into being of the zodiac system.

Although the classical 'World-soul' or Logos of the Greeks, can be defined as the 'solar-word', yet Rudolf Steiner explains that it can also be defined as meaning the great, zodiacal Logos.[40] This 'Self of the Cosmos' is the highest aspect of 'Christ'; it is the Son, or Second Person of the Trinity, (a second Logos). Rudolf Steiner taught that, "It is such a mightily evolved cosmic being that even for the highest clairvoyant consciousness, It remains ineffable. No matter how high the initiate may be able to raise their consciousness, they can only comprehend a small part of It."[41] An archive note gives a further description of this sublime being

Christ :

Physical body = the Sun
Etheric body = the 7 planets
Astral body = the 12 zodiac signs
The I = is beyond even these[42]

I will refer to this very important note again, below.
The other usage of the term 'das Welten-Ich' refers to a mysterious aspect of the Christ-impulse, a being who derives from the hierarchies, but who is not always clearly identified. Rudolf Steiner generally declined in lectures to reveal just what aspect of the Christ-impulse is meant here; he referred to this being as the macrocosmic self of the human being. On one occasion he simply stated that "with the Sun and Earth a very hidden and mysterious being is associated".[43]

---

[40] Lecture cycle on The Gospel of St. Matthew, lecture 12, and on The Gospel of St. John, lecture 1.
[41] Ga 118, p. 21, a lect. of 13. April 1913, Rome.
[42] Archive note published in GA 150, as an addendum.
[43] Lecture; From Buddha to Christ, of 25th May 1909, in GA 109/111.

Normally, the term "Christ' refers to the foremost of the Sun-spirits, or Spirits of Form (Exusiai). However in his Esoteric Lessons Rudolf Steiner revealed that the 'Self of the Cosmos', which is also an aspect of the inmost of self of the human being, can be viewed as an expression of the Christ within the interweaving of two ranks of hierarchical beings higher than the Sun-spirits or Powers. These beings are the Mights and also the sublime Seraphim. This aspect of the Christ-Impulse is concerned especially with the spiritualizing of the 'sheaths' of humanity, with enlivening what is formed and rigid. In particular, he refers to a Seraphim, as the 'Self of the Cosmos'.

So, this Being is clearly a higher divinity — a Seraph — and is the second meaning of the term "the Self of the Cosmos" (or "Cosmic I"). However, the activity of this Seraphic aspect of the 'Self of the Cosmos' is interwoven with that of the Sun-Spirit Christ. The concept of "spiritualizing of the 'sheaths' of humanity" refers to the need for the physical, etheric and astral bodies to spiritualise, and not become hardened. As they spiritualize, the threefold human spirit emerges.

From the context of this section B, it is clear that the expression 'the Self of the Cosmos' (das Welten-Ich) refers primarily to the great cosmic Logos, in whose activities there is an interweaving of the above aspects of the Christ-Impulse. But it is also clear from the solar nuance of the expression, "let from the east be enkindled", that both the Seraphic and Sun-Spirit aspects of Christ are involved. So, both of the entities designated by the expression, "the Self of the Cosmos' are involved here.

However, there is an interaction of these beings with the solar Christ. In 1924 Rudolf Steiner explained that the Life-Spirit of the solar Christ permeates the Earth's aura, although it can not be exerting an influence so obviously or as quickly as the 'Spirit-Self' of Christ. The aspect of Christ which is more tangibly active with the Earth and humanity is the equivalent of what we could term, his Spirit-Self. Whereas the former process bestows sanctified soul-light on the earth, the latter process will gradually re-enliven the earth's ethers and also each individual human ether-body.[44]

To the extent that the meditant spiritualises her or his ether body, the faculty of Inspiration arises. In the deeper elucidations of this mystery to members of the Esoteric School (1908), he indicated that this receiving of the Life-Spirit by humanity requires the efficacy of the Mights, and the Seraphic aspect of Christ.[45] Illustration Five can give valuable indications for meditation on why the Mights (Spirits of Movement) are also involved in this specific spiritualising of our ether-body, that is, the development of Life-Spirit.

The illustration shows that the Mights have Life-Spirit (or Buddhi) as their lowest 'member'. This is significant here, as it means that they are rising above it, or out-growing it, so to speak. The consequence of such an out-growing of a 'member' by an Hierarchical Being, (and all ranks are slowly out-growing their lowest 'member',

---

[44] See lecture in Karmic Relationships series; London, 27th August 1924.

[45] This material was provided only to those souls admitted to that school, as he had assessed them as capable of assimilating such revelations (and hence the material was not meant to be published).

towards the end of an aeon) is that these forces will tend to enhance the development of this in the next lowest rank of being.

In this case, the Hierarchical beings below are the Sun-spirits. Further, the focus of consciousness of the Mights is the "Son' stage of consciousness. This stage, as the illustration shows, is seven stages above the ether-body level, from that level of being, the ether can be worked upon in a formative manner. Any level of consciousness which is seven stages above a specific level, exercises an influence similar to that of the forces which created the former.

The Self of the Cosmos as the Logos, manifests through the rhythms of the celestial bodies, and within "the on-surging deeds" of those Hierarchical beings who are evolving this aspect of the cosmos. These rhythms have a vital role in the maintaining of the consciousness of the Earth in its various levels, and with this process, the divine Seraphic Christ and the Life-Spirit of the solar Christ, as the incarnate Spirit of the Earth, is active.

B9 unite your own self

In terms of the symbolism of the foundation stone, these processes mean that the human being as the smaller, second dodecahedron, takes on life and form, following the pattern of the zodiacal cosmic dodecahedron. We noted above that the Self of the Cosmos, or Logos (called 'Christ' in the archive note,) is cosmically understood as;

Physical body = the Sun
Etheric body = the 7 planets
Astral body   = the 12 zodiac signs
The I   = is beyond even these

This outline can be compared with the following outline of the cosmic origins of the human being, as defined in a lecture given in 1921, where Rudolf Steiner summarizes the lecture in this way:

Human being[46]
Physical body = echo of the zodiac
I = perception of the echo of the zodiac
Etheric body = echo of the movement of the planets
Astral body = experience of the movement of the planets

Meditation upon these two correspondences of the nature of humanity and of the Christ-Logos is a valuable aid in working with the dodecahedron foundation stone. The implication of line b9 is an experience of merging with the above divine being, whom we could refer to as the Logos-permeated cosmic Christ.

The implication of these two brief summaries of the 'members' of the human being and of the great Self of the Cosmos is that we are a microcosm of the macrocosm. In section A, the human soul has realized that the core of its being has its origin in God (via hierarchical deities). In section B, the human soul experiences union with the Logos via hierarchical beings associated with the active pulsing, rhythmical life-quickening Son.

b11/12 Then you truly shall be feeling within the dynamics of the human soul
These lines are difficult to render poetically, but this version accurately conveys the meaning. Its meaning becomes clearer if one renders it as, "Then you truly

---

[46] Lecture of 18th Dec. 1921, in GA 209.

shall be feeling within the <u>authentic</u> dynamics of the human soul."

The phrase, if translated precisely is, 'Then you truly shall be feeling within the efficacy of the human soul", but efficacy would occur too often if also used here. The meaning is, as with the same line in the other sections, that once a person has developed these initiatory states of awareness within the spiritual spheres of the cosmic human spirit, then that person is, paradoxically, functioning within the quintessential human reality.

The true, authentic dynamics are then awakened in the person. Thus the implication of this line is that our dynamics are not fully authentic, not fully human until this happens. This of course redefines the human being as primarily a spiritual being, rather than a person whose dynamics are limited to the elemental forces that predominate in earthly life.

b13 **From horizon unto horizon**
This line has been translated into the phrase "the encircling Round", a formulation which is too vague. The German term, Umkreis, means 'circumference' or 'extent' or 'circuit', and refers here to the periphery of the globe of the Earth. It is clear from R. Steiner's use of the term, "Umkreis", that this correlates to his meaning of this term; "in the Umkreis of the Earth the Christ left his Life-Spirit……in the atmosphere of the earth He had his Life-Spirit…"[47]

We noted earlier that the three sections invoke a form of world-cross. Forces from the Father-God arise up from inside the Earth, and forces from the Holy Spirit descend.

---

[47] See ref. 16.

Here in this middle section, forces are efficacious on us horizontally. So, then one has to extend this idea of the over-arching firmament or periphery of the globe into the human existential sphere.

From the viewpoint of a person living on the surface of the Earth, this periphery is the current horizon merging into a succession of changing horizons that curve downwards ahead of you, and to the left and the right as well, as one imagines the movement across the surface of the Earth.

The expression, 'from horizon unto horizon' accurately translates the primary meaning of the word here. As Rudolf Steiner explained in lectures on art, "the human being experiences the Umkreis of the Earth with the middle section, (the heart) area, with the feelings."[48] This middle section of the great verse appeals to the refining of our feelings. The ambiguous word 'feelings' has both meanings here. The emotions or desires, and also sensing with the body's sense organs of either the physical or etheric worlds.

These archetypal, spiritual ether-energies now weave through the Earth's atmospheric ether layers, which are identified and described in detail in, "Living A Spiritual Year". Rudolf Steiner describes them as "streaming over the horizon… powerful streams of ethereal energy", which maintain the life of the planet. (1906) That this nuance is indeed the case with this line, is confirmed by his explanation of this phrase, given just prior to speaking this verse, "The Christ-Power which weaves over

---

[48] From GA 291, "Das Wesen der Farben" p. 179. Lect. June 2nd 1923

everything across the horizon, encircling the Earth in the atmosphere, and which is active in our breathing…"

However it is also clear that there is also a nuance of something more than global in this term, implying that the 'circumferencing circuit' extends into space. That is, it includes the wonderful cosmic rhythms to which our planet is subject from the motion of the Sun around the heavens, that is, through the zodiac.

Since rhythmical processes are a major element of this middle section of the great verse, and involve the Logos, the phrase also refers to Sun and Earth moving in space against the zodiac background, and the rhythms they thus create, which interact with the rhythms of life in nature that fill our own local horizon.

This cosmic nuance is to be found in Rudolf Steiner's lectures when he speaks of the human soul having a connection to the World-Soul (or "self of the cosmos"). He explains in such lectures that there exists a dynamic in our rhythmical systems, created by the Self of the Cosmos. This derives from rhythmical interactions between the pulsing of our heart and lung and astronomical movements, through which our breathing has a rhythm which is identical to a major cosmic rhythm of the sun around the zodiac. This refers to an awe-inspiring cosmic rhythm, and affirms that the meaning of the verse is one that points to the cosmic movement of Sun and Earth.

The rhythm linking the human soul and the World-soul, as it is called in ancient Greek texts is described by him as follows:
        in 1 minute we breathe 18 times
        in 1 hour   we breathe 1080 times

in 1 day   we breathe 25,920 times

So, in one day, we breathe 25,920 times. 72 years is 1 classically defined earth life-span in the Bible, but in 72 years there are 25,920 days. The Sun moves through the zodiac signs, slowly slipping backwards through each sign, when observed from the Earth on the same day, each year.

So, its position is now in Pisces, when observed on 21st March, but in the future it will have moved when seen on March 21st into Aquarius. The Sun, in this slow, almost imperceptible cosmic motion takes 72 years to move 1 degree of the 360 degree circle of the heavens around us. So, in one classical life-span of 72 years, the Sun has moved one degree.

The sky is divided into 12 divisions or signs of the zodiac, each of which are 30 degrees in size. The Sun takes 2,160 years to move through each zodiac sign. In 2,160 years, there are 25,920 months. How long does the Sun take to complete one of its days, that is one circuit around the 12 zodiac signs ? It takes 25,920 years ! (On the etheric level; physically its journey is slightly variable.)

Now, the movement of this Sun around the Earth occurs across the background of the zodiac. In each spring equinox, solar energies with their accompanying zodiac influences are able to flow into the Earth's aura. This is a process which for the planet may be likened to an in-breathing of celestial forces, so there is a cosmic interchange of forces taking place. That is, a process similar to the interchange of forces that occurs when we breathe in and out, exchanging substances and etheric forces with the atmosphere.

So, summarizing:

In one Earth day, we breathe	25,920 times
The Sun completes one solar day in	25,920 years
The Sun occupies a zodiac sign for	25,920 months
The Sun moves $1°$ in 72 years, but 72 years, or one classical life-span, occupies	25,920 days.

Our feeling-life is truly a microcosm of the macrocosm. Our feeling-sensing life — made possible by the beat of heart and lung — pulses in direct correlation to the rhythm that exists between the Self of the Cosmos and the Earth. In this rhythm, the Self of the Cosmos is interacting with the Logos-permeated cosmic Christ, who is the indwelling Spirit of the Earth.

b13 bestowing Grace

It is actually the case that the word 'Grace' refers to the same spiritual force as the Life-Spirit, hence general expressions such as, 'blessing the soul' are quite incorrect. Rudolf Steiner explained that this New Testament term, 'Grace' is the same as what Theosophists call Buddhi, and what in anthroposophy is normally called 'the Life-spirit'; namely the divine source of 'life'.[49]

These terms mean the actual Devachanic spiritual reality from which the ether energies derive. Hence the meaning of these lines is a quite specific enlivening and spiritualizing of our life-energies (ether-body) which is bestowed on us. This process occurs through deliberate transformative actions undertaken within these cosmic-earthly rhythms by the now incarnate Logos-enfilled cosmic Christ. It is not an indefinable 'blessing' action, but literally an 'en-gracing' process.

---

[49] Ref. 14, page 267.

This process occurs especially strongly through two rhythmical processes, one of which occurs during the seasonal cycle. In brief, in each wintertime, spiritual forces that flow through those "powerful streams of ether energy" mentioned above, from which Grace actually derives, penetrate deep into the Earth's interior, drawn in by the 'in-breathing' of the hemisphere's auric energies in winter.

This divine solar energy is activated in the hemisphere during its wintertime, and is the esoteric reason for the birth of the divine light being celebrated in ancient and current religions at the winter solstice. The other occasion when the soul contacts the stream of 'Grace' is in the rhythm of the day. Every evening we pass into sleep and rise up through the ether-streams pulsing above the horizon, flowing from east to west. To the extent that the soul is in a tangible spiritualization process, the ether-body can absorb some of these Grace energies.

The first cosmic rhythm, the wintertime one, has existed since the Earth began to rotate on it axis, the second rhythm, of being immersed in the Grace forces at night, has only existed since the cosmic Christ "incarnated" at Golgotha, and became the regent of the Earth. The spiritualizing of our life-energies assists the meditant to achieve Contemplation, the term used by Rudolf Steiner as the second phase of the meditative process. From this Contemplation process the faculty of "Inspiration" or *Cosmic-Spiritual Consciousness* (not just *Psychic-Image Consciousness* or *Imagination*) arises. But practise in becoming sensitive to the spiritual forces inherent in our environment is necessary for this process. Following the cycle of the year and its rhythms is an excellent way to practise this.

b 17 **Let from the east be enkindled**
This refers to precisely those powerful ether-streams mentioned earlier, which pulse across the horizon, moving from east to west. It is a vital element in the anthroposophical world-view that the spiritual manifests itself indirectly through the phenomena of the physical-etheric, but the temptation is natural to separate the divine entirely from the created world.

Hence the idea that the ether-body becomes "engraced" through the life-spirit forces in the rhythmical efficacy of the ether currents of the planet, whether at the winter solstice or during (less powerfully) each night can be difficult at first to grasp. But this is the meaning of the line.

The details of the Earth's energy-aura is also a little-known subject. Rudolf Steiner mentioned "mighty ether-streams (in the atmosphere) which flow from east to west". In this lecture, he also spoke of how the second hierarchy, the Dominions, Mights and Powers, that is, precisely the same Beings invoked in this middle section of the great verse, are actually within these ether streams, moving across the periphery of the horizon, from east to west.

He explains that we are exposed to these streams as we move up through the atmosphere each night in sleep. These beings of the second hierarchy are described as "permeating their nexus in a grace-bestowing manner, and of this influence from the Second Hierarchy, it is said, "this most definitely makes an impact on our soul-life." [50]

---

[50] R.Steiner, lecture cycle, Mystery Centres, lect. 25.Nov 1923.

These energies pulse in a rhythmical manner, affected by the seasonal in-breathing and out-breathing of the hemisphere. The cosmic Christ and the Self of the Cosmos are present in these life-forces of the Earth and exert a vital activity in them. However, in contrast to these energies which flow from the east, and which help to enliven incarnate consciousness by etherealizing the physical-flesh body, there are also the opposite energies; those from the western horizon.

b18 What from the west is formed

From the west flow ether and astral forces deriving from the Moon, which give concrete form to life on Earth. In Esoteric Lessons Rudolf Steiner refers to "the forming, rounding lunar power, which can lead to rigidity, numbness" (1913), and hence he assigned Ahriman to the west, for the purpose of esoteric contemplation of the world-cross (the four directions and their astral forces). These indications refer to the malignant aspect of the Moon.

The Moon has two aspects to it, one is very wholesome, nurturing life on Earth, the other is indeed ahrimanic. The theme of the ahrimanic nature of the lunar forces can be found throughout the lectures of Rudolf Steiner. For example in April 1921, he referred to the conflict between social impulses in the human sphere that seek to make humans into automatons and those which seek to stimulate enthusiasm and love. The hardening impulses were associated with lunar forces from the west, but the enlivening impulses with the east.

It is through the "Gate of the Moon" that our past karma brings us into the solid, material earthly world. Our physical body benumbs our ability to respond to the rhythmical ethereal pulse of these ether streams that flow from the east, and which carry within them divine Life-Spirit forces from the cosmic Christ. These are complex issues, the main purpose of the verse is to allow each meditant to intuitively find their way to these truths, one does not need the detailed knowledge beforehand. A useful meditative aphorism here, which comes from the Esoteric School (1910) is the brief and enigmatic phrase, "from the east resounds the holy Word".

b20 In Christo Morimur

This Latin phrase is one of three which form a meditative maxim created by Christian Rosenkreutz. It means literally, 'in Christ we die' (the noun is in the 'accusative' case). But, this phrase can imply a negative sense, namely that we humans all lose our life in Christ. This expression, with its allusions to St. Paul's teachings in his epistle to the Romans, actually intends to say that once we have died, we find ourselves having an existence in Christ.

This deep truth can be applied to a dying of the personal-lower self and the emergence of the higher self, or to life after death. Both these meaning are implied by Rudolf Steiner here, as his commentary in line 21 indicates, "in Christ, death becomes life". To give this a more positive nuance I have used the rendering, 'into Christ we die' (the 'dative' case). This second translation allows the phrase to convey its profound and inspiring meanings.

In Rudolf Steiner's commentary (line 21) or rather, paraphrased translation; "In Christ, death becomes life", and in the following lines, an implication is hinted at, which has to do with our incarnate existence, and how this can be raised to a higher level. Namely it refers to an enlivening power of the Second Hierarchy, flowing from the east, as an expression of the will of Christ, which opposes the deadening, hardening forces of Ahriman, who utilises the malignant, stagnant lunar energies flowing from the west.

This is not a theoretical matter, for in some millennia to come these presently subtle dynamics will intensify. The activity of the solar forces against the hardening lunar powers is a continuous process. Rudolf Steiner reports that these ahrimanic lunar powers will take on an ever more potent and malignant role, but active against these powers will be the cosmic Christ and the spiritual beings who produce the two hemisphere's seasonal cycle.

It is the intention of the Christ-Impulse to ensure that most of humanity will not become the victims of a hardened, dying Earth. This process of becoming imbued with enlivening Life-Spirit forces also occurs every wintertime, for each hemisphere. It happens during the days after the solstice, at which time some Life-Spirit forces are bestowed on humanity during sleep.[51]

The interweaving of these great cosmic and geo-centric forces constitutes a re-birth of the soul-spiritual part of the earth. These lines refer primarily to the Earth's astral substance and etheric energies are being renewed, from divine-spiritual (Devachanic) sources. The interpretation of these lines as referring to activity of European esoteric streams historically, (as is done in some commentaries), is an exploration of a lesser, historical implication of the above lines.

---

[51] See ref. 15, chapter 258, 259.

SECTION C: This is an exploration of the dynamics involved, both in oneself and in the spiritual realms, in developing Imagination, or what I call *Psychic Image Consciousness*, the first of the three states of initiate consciousness and the easiest to attain.

c4 **Cosmic-Thoughts:**
Literally 'cosmos-thoughts', this refers to the "imaginations" or thought-forms concerning the structure and purpose of the cosmos, as produced by the divine hierarchical beings. These thought-forms infuse the higher worlds with a intense radiance. See commentary to lines 14,15.

c5 **Spirit-Beholding:**
You may feel to this to be an archaic term, but there are not many possible alternatives. However, 'Perceiving' is an adequate alternative, 'seeing' or 'recognizing' are less accurate and less effective. In any event the meaning of this phrase is to think in the holistic sense, wherein *Psychic-Image Consciousness* or *Imagination occurs,* so one's thoughts are now being registered as they emerge in the ether body, and not only after the brain has grasped them, and hollowed them out. The perceptions may be registered as either these subtle impressions, or even directly as astral vision.

The result of this is that one's consciousness becomes receptive to the etheric-astral reality of an idea, beyond its mere mental representation formed through the brain, The meditant is moving towards seeing the spiritual reality — the etheric-astral imagination.

c10 **That the will may be free**
Notice here the significance of this line, that it is through diligent meditation, and heart-centred study of spiritual

truths, that the meditant gradually achieves a high goal of spiritual development, namely <u>freedom in the will.</u> This implies the freeing of the volitional forces from all that seeks to keep a person inwardly enslaved in the will. Practical, intensified will-forces are especially developed through this reclusive, introspective activity of meditating (after some time has passed).

c14 the Spirit's cosmic thoughts, invoking light…
Here a wider view of the term, 'the Holy Spirit' is implied, namely, the activity of all higher spirits who work with the striving human soul, is holy. The consciousness of spiritual beings endows them with a special radiance. Since the Spirit's cosmic-thoughts are radiant by nature, this process invokes light into the world of humankind.

As the (holy) spirit approaches the meditant's soul, radiant light simply enters with it, once the Spiritual Beholding (*Imagination: Psychic-Image Consciousness*) occurs. Rudolf Steiner defines what he means by his expression 'the Cosmic Thoughts' (Weltgedanken) in various lectures. For example, "…cosmic thoughts are that, according to which divine powers have created the world…they pervade the cosmos as rays of (etheric-astral) energy". A further description is, "cosmic thinking is that true thinking (i.e., consciousness state) which pervades the cosmos like rays of energy in it."[52]

He also describes "the divine cosmic thoughts, according to which the world was created… great cosmic thoughts, efficacious, but usually hidden." They are described as "having created the physical body over ages, thus in the

---

[52] R. Steiner: G/A 93:204 & G/A 84: 78-83.

body, cosmic wisdom is slumbering."[53] These thoughts are also efficacious in the ethers…imaginative thoughts are derived from the cosmic ether." [54]

Published translations have 'beseech' or 'pray', instead of the word 'invoke', but this not applicable here for two reasons. Firstly, from the above considerations, it is clear that the cosmic 'thoughts' (that is, consciousness) of Devachanic spiritual Beings naturally permeate Creation with their light, so 'beseeching' them to do this would be superfluous.

Furthermore, the thing from which action is expected, the object of the verb 'erflehen', is not a specific entity, but rather these cosmic thoughts, not a specific hierarchical Being. These cosmic thoughts obviously cannot be beseeched to do anything, hence a non-individuated process is meant, not a beseeching which has to refer to something individual or personalized.

As dictionaries from Rudolf Steiner's life-time point out, a century ago, when the German verb 'erflehen' refers to a general quality, not a <u>specific</u> person or divinity, then 'invoke' is the more correct translation. The point of this section of the verse is to affirm that through developing astral consciousness, by practising Spirit-Beholding, the meditant will experience the illumination of consciousness (and spread this around himself), through the radiance which is naturally invoked into the world by the radiant cosmic thought-forms of the divine beings.

---

[53] R. Steiner G/A 96, lect 12.April 1907, "Easter, the festival of spiritual re-birth".
[54] R. Steiner G/A 84, p. 81.

The world's being can thusly become more radiant. As Rudolf Steiner noted in his preparatory material for the Esoteric School, "the thoughts-universe should think within our ether-body, then the human being is placing his ether body in the correct harmony with the universal cosmic thoughts."[55] The adoption here of an ecclesiastical ambience, as in 'hold sway', for this sentence is again, in a parallel with the term, 'walten', out of place.

c20: **Per Spiritum Sanctum Reviviscimus**
This means literally, 'by the Holy Spirit we are resurrected', and like the other two Rosicrucian verses has other profoundly esoteric meanings, but the nuance emphasised here concerns the effect of attaining illumination by the cosmic thoughts of the hierarchies.

SECTION D
This refers to the uniting of the Sun-Spirit, the central life-bestowing deity in our solar system, with the Earth. However, it is central in anthroposophical knowledge, that the sublime Logos was present in the Sun-god Christ. The uniting of this divine reality to the Earth's aura commenced with the Baptism in the Jordan, and was completed in the Crucifixion and Resurrection events.

d2: **the Spirit of the Cosmos**
This German expression, 'der Weltengeist', has not always been understood, and at times is mistranslated as 'the spirit-light of the world'; an almost meaningless phrase. The phrase, translated into English, is actually, the Light of the Cosmic-Spirit (or Spirit of the Cosmos).

---

[55] This esoteric archive material, is in GA 267, p145.

This expression was used by the great initiate in three different ways.

Firstly for God, as regent of the universe; that is, the first of the three Persons of the Trinity, the "creative primal power of creation". Secondly, for the Sun-Spirit as governing body of our solar system, and especially in particular, the central Beings of the Sun – the cosmic, solar Christ. It could be used in the broader sense of the Pleroma, or the seven Elohim. And thirdly Rudolf Steiner used it as a designation for the Spirit of the Earth, in the sense of the indwelling cosmic Christ.

In this verse, Rudolf Steiner wishes it to mean primarily, but not exclusively, the Ruler of the Sun-sphere, the highest of the Spirits of Form, namely the cosmic Christ. However, there is a close interweaving (that is, ontological affinity) between the Father-God (the First Person of the primal Trinity) and the "Sun-Spirit Christ". Especially when, as here, one is to think of the interweaving of the sublime Logos within this solar 'cosmic Christ'.

That a 'ray' of the Father-God is an integral aspect of the divine Light that entered the Earth at the mystery of Golgotha will be emphasized more by initiates in future ages. It is too difficult for normal consciousness to gain real insight into the Father-God. Hence Rudolf Steiner normally presents the Golgotha event as especially the bringing the radiance of the cosmic Christ, imbued with the Logos, to the Earth.

But, as we have noted, reference is made, 'godly light'. So, this line in the verse allows many deep nuances about the supernal light to be meditated. One's attention is drawn to the nature of God, and the nature of the spiritual forces pertaining to the cosmic Christ that began to enter the Earth at the Baptism in the Jordan, and which was completed at the Resurrection.

That there is a close connection of the Logos aspect of Christ and the Father God is a central truth of Christian theology. But this affinity of the primal God with the Christ-impulse is clearly shown in Scripture. For example, where the cosmic Christ, speaking through Christ-Jesus, says, "I came from the Father, and I have come into the world; and now, I am leaving the world and am going to the Father." (John 16.28).

This same truth with its immense implications as to the sublime sanctity of the Mystery of Golgotha is also expressed in John 20.21, "As you, Father are in me, and I am in You, may they also be in us, so that the world may believe that You sent me."

It may be helpful here to include definitions of the 'Weltengeist' and the two other persons of the Trinity by Rudolf Steiner. Although very brief, they are very useful to confirm the identity of this Being. This information comes from archive material published in volumes concerned with the Esoteric School. His notes as published in volumes 265-267 record the following:

> 1:*Father God / First Logos*
> the Cosmos-Spirit (Weltengeist), the cosmic Will, whose Will is efficacious from itself...the creative primal-power of the cosmos. The 'Will-manifesting' spirit of God, the First Logos, the bearer of the all-encompassing cosmic laws, the bearer of the sublime Good.
>
> 2: *The Son/ Second Logos*

> *the Cosmos-Soul (Weltenseele), which possesses a sensing that streams out from it...the creative cosmic love, the Second Logos, it had created the organ for feeling in the human being*
>
> 3: *The Holy Spirit / Third Logos*
> *The Cosmic Thinking, cosmic Intelligence, it had created the organ for thought in the human being.*

These note-book entries identify the 'Cosmos-Spirit' as the First Person of the primal Trinity – when the triune Godhead is being referred to. However, in our verse, it points especially to the cosmic Sun-god Christ. It is also the case that these two deities are closely interlinked.

So, the main meaning of this phrase is to the cosmic Christ, who is also referred to as the 'Weltengeist'. At Golgotha, the primary event is often described by Rudolf Steiner, as the descent of the cosmic Christ into the Earth. Hence the phrase, "the light of the cosmic Spirit' refers mainly to Christ.

But, as we have noted above, in the 'Spirit of the Cosmos' or Christ is a ray from the Logos, or second person of the Trinity. Since the Father God is closely linked to the Logos, then one may also meditate here on the implication that there is to some extent a presence of the Father God in the radiant light which flooded the Earth's aura at the sacrifice of Golgotha.

The broad description of this given in lines d10 & d11 "**Light divine** (or, 'godly light'), **Christ Sun**" make it clear that the spiritual light that entered our planet at the "primal Christmas" from the cosmic Christ, has both a solar nature and a 'godly' nature.

d4 **Darkness of Night** (or **Deep darkness**)
The literal translation is, 'darkness of night', but the expression "Nacht-Dunkel" can often mean a deep darkness, not necessarily the literal darkness of night time. If one uses 'deep darkness', then the meaning can expand beyond a darkness caused by the physical absence of the sun.

d5 **Day-radiant light** (or **Sun-radiant light**)
The usual translation, "day-radiant light" is poetically a valid translation and contrasts with 'Darkness of Night'; and is fully correct to the German. But the brightness of day derives from the sunlight not the day, and the great Sun-spirit is now inaugurating a new epoch.

d16: **resolve**
This is literally, 'will to purposefully direct'.

With regard to the seven extracts that are to be used on the relevant day of the week, please note that I have included the line 'Human Soul !' for the Tuesday section, but these two words should begin each day's sections. One can imagine that these words are being spoken to oneself from the spiritual worlds.

The Sunday section may cause some confusion. It consists of recalling to mind – or rather letting silently resound within the soul – the three invocations to soul exertion (e.g., practise Spirit-Remembering) and then bringing these into connection with the very last part of the great verse, "that good may come of what in our hearts is laid down".

The meditant will find that it is very worthwhile to read the two small booklets published by the Steiner publishing companies in either the UK or USA on this verse. Both of these are titled, 'The Foundation Stone meditation', one is the text of Rudolf Steiner's explanation of the verse, the other is a commentary by F. Zeylmans van Emmichoven, and is of value for further ideas.

******

The question as to whether the Christmas Re-founding process was actually successful in bringing about a full and permanent union of the Anthroposophical Society with the Anthroposophical movement, is not under consideration in this book. The Rudolf Steiner Archives administration has published material from various anthroposophists on this subject which includes statements made in private conversations by Rudolf Steiner, where he tells them that the re-founding of the society was not successful.

Members of the Society's executive (the 'Vorstand') at Dornach have published arguments to the contrary. What is undeniable in my experience, is that meditation on the Foundation Stone verse does indeed allow one to unite one's soul with the spiritual source of the anthroposophical movement.

****

7   The German Text

Menschenseele !
Du lebest in den Gliedern,
Die dich durch die Raumeswelt
In das Geistesmeereswesen tragen:
Übe *Geist-Erinnern*
In Seelentiefen,
Wo in waltendem
Weltenschöpfer-Sein
Das eigne Ich
Im Gottes-Ich
Erweset;
Und wirst wahrhaft *leben*
Im Menschen-Welten-Wesen.

Denn es waltet der Vater-Geist der Höhen
In den Weltentiefen Sein-erzeugend.
Ihr Kräfte-Geister !
– Seraphim, Cherubim, Throne –
Lasset aus den Höhen erklingen
Was in den Tiefen das Echo findet:
Dieses spricht:
Ex Deo Nascimur.
Aus dem Göttlichen weset die Menschheit.
Das hören die Elementargeister in Ost, West, Nord, Sud:
Menchen mögen es hören.

Menschenseele !
Du lebest in dem Herzens-Lungen-Schlage,
Der dich durch den Zeitenrhythmus
Ins eigene Seelenwesensfühlen leitet:
Übe *Geist-Besinnen*
Im Seelengleichgewichte,
Wo die wogenden
Welten-Werde-Taten
Das eigene Ich
Dem Welten-Ich
Vereinen;
Und du wirst wahrhaft *fühlen*
Im Menschen-Seelen-Wirken.

Denn es waltet der Christus-Wille im Umkreis
In den Weltenrhythmen Seelen-begnadend:
Ihr Lichtes-Geister !
 – Kyriotetes, Dynameis, Exusiai –
Lasset vom Ostern befeuern,
Was durch den Westen sich formet,
Dieses spricht:
In Christo morimur
In dem Christus wird Leben der Tod.
Das hören die Elementargeister in Ost, West, Nord, Süd:
Menchen mögen es hören.

Menschenseele !
Du lebest im ruhenden Haupte,
Das dir aus Ewigkeitsgründen
Die Weltgedanken erschließet:
Übe *Geist-Erschauen*
In Gedanken-Ruhe,
Wo die ew'gen Götterziele
Welten-Wesens-Licht
Dem eignen Ich
Zu freiem Wollen
Schenken:
Und wirst wahrhaft *denken*
In Menschen-Geistes-Gründen.

Denn es waltet des Geistes Weltgedanken
Im Weltenwesen Licht-erflehend.
Ihr Seelen-Geister !
– Archai, Archangeloi, Angeloi –
Lasset aus den Tiefen erbitten,
Was in den Höhen erhöret wird;
Dieses spricht:
Per spiritum sanctum reviviscimus.
In des Geistes Weltgedanken erwachet die Seele.
Das hören die Elementargeister in Ost, West, Nord, Süd:
Menchen mögen es hören.

In der Zeiten Wende
Trat das Welten-Geistes-Licht
In den irdischenWesenstrom;

Nacht-Dunkel hatte ausgewaltet;
Taghelles Licht
Erstrahlte in Menschenseelen:
Licht,
Das erwärmet
Die armen Hirtenherzen;
Licht, das erleuchtet
Die weisen Königshäupter.

Göttliches Licht,
Christus-Sonne,
Erwärme Unsere Herzen,
Erleuchte Unsere Häupter;
Daß gut werde,
Was wir
Aus Herzen gründen,
Was wir
Aus Häuptern zielvoll führen wollen.

Copyright acknowledgements:
The German text of the Address and verse by Rudolf Steiner was published by the Verlag der Rudolf Steiner-Nachlassverwaltung, Dornach, 1963, in GA vol. 260.

The text of the ritual address of 1913 exists in a manuscript, a copy of which is in my library (the text given in Grosse has a key verb missing). Quotes from or references to, Esoteric School material, comes from unpublished manuscripts in my library, except where indicated.

The English version of the material concerning the Christmas Re-founding Conference (in GA vol. 260), is published as "The Christmas Conference" by Anthroposophic Press, Hudson, N.Y., 1990.

Illustrations Copyright notice:

Illustration 1: copyright by the Anthroposophischen Gesellschaft in Deutschland, and reproduced with their kind permission.
Illustration 2 and 3: copyright by the Verlag am Goetheanum, and reproduced with their kind permission

Illustrations 4 and 5: copyright by Adrian Anderson, 2002.

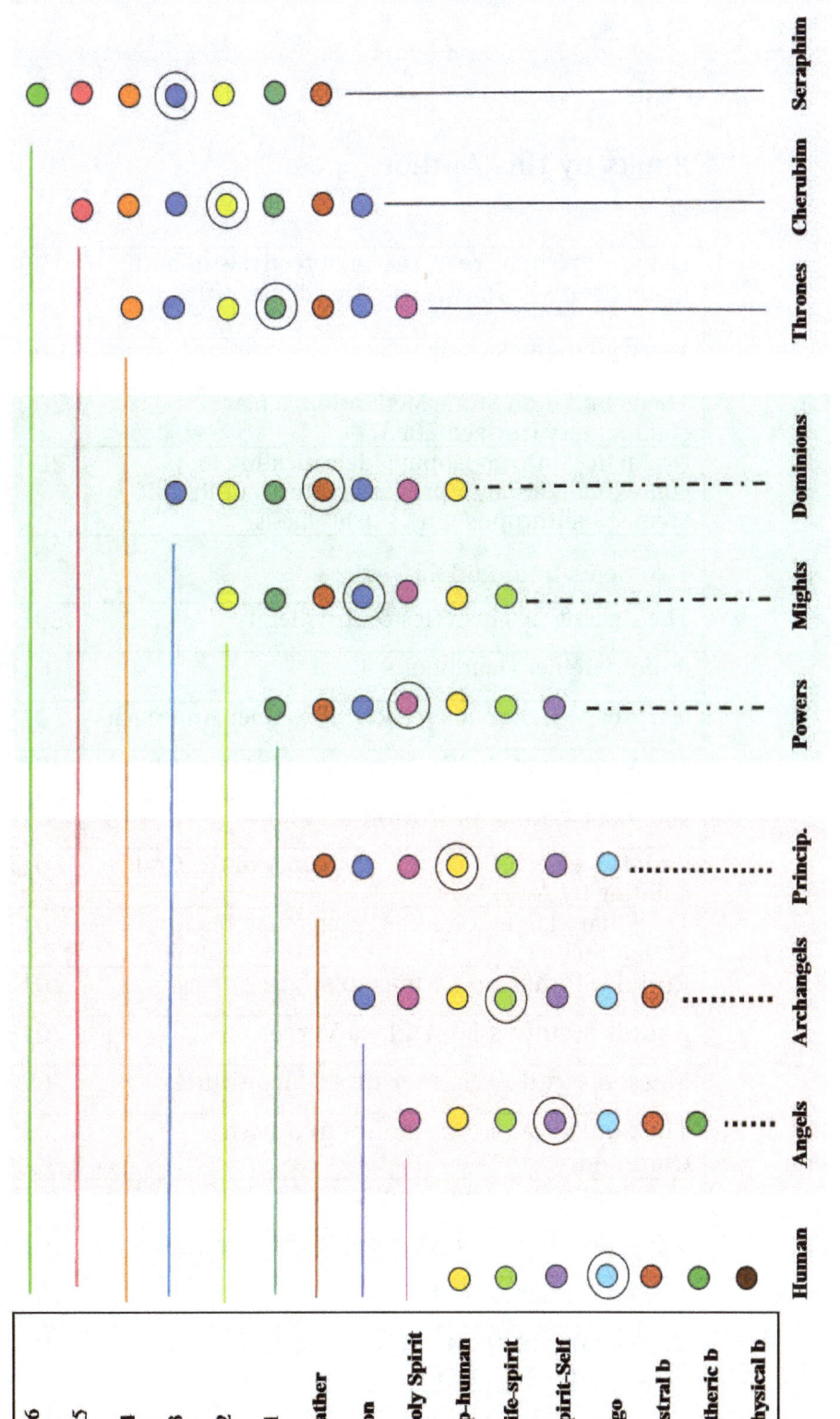

The nature of each hierarchy A dot with a circle around it = focus of consciousness of that rank of being. Left: names of levels of awareness of awareness above Spirit-human, from R. Steiner, not referring to the Trinity, but the Trinity is reflected in these levels of awareness.

Books by this Author

Living a Spiritual Year: seasonal festivals in both hemispheres (new, expanded edition, 2016)	1992
The Way to the Sacred	2003
The Foundation Stone Meditation: a new commentary (revised 2023)	2005
Dramatic Anthroposophy: Identification and contextualization of primary features of Rudolf Steiner's anthroposophy. (PhD thesis)	2005
Two Gems from Rudolf Steiner	2014
The Hellenistic Mysteries & Christianity	2014
Rudolf Steiner Handbook	2014
Horoscope Handbook – a Rudolf Steiner Approach	2015
The Meaning of the Goetheanum Windows	2016
The Lost Zodiac of Rudolf Steiner	2016
Rudolf Steiner's Esoteric Christianity in the Grail painting by Anna May	2017
The Vidar Flame Column – its meaning from Rudolf Steiner	2017
Rudolf Steiner on Leonardo's *Last Supper*	2017
Rudolf Steiner's First Class Verses	2018
Blessed - Rudolf Steiner on the Beatitudes	2018
The Soul's Calendar - annotated with Commentary	2019
The Soul's Calendar - pocket edition	2019
The Apocalyptic Seals from Rudolf Steiner	2020
The Mysteries of Ephesos	2021
The Gospel of John; an Initiatory Pathway Translation & Commentary	2022

Also, under the pen-name Damien Pryor:	
The nature & origin of the Tropical Zodiac	2011
Stonehenge	2011
Lalibela	2011
The Externsteine	2011
The Great Pyramid & the Sphinx	2011